Exposing False Spiritual Leaders

Exposing False Spiritual Leaders

by
John MacArthur, Jr.

WORD OF GRACE COMMUNICATIONS
P.O. Box 4000
Panorama City, CA 91412

All Scripture quotations, unless noted otherwise, are from the *New Scofield Reference Bible*, King James Version. Copyright © 1967 by Oxford University Press, Inc. Reprinted by permission.

Library of Congress Cataloging in Publication Data

MacArthur, John F.
    Exposing false spiritual leaders.

    (John MacArthur's Bible studies)
    Includes index.
    1. Bible. N.T. Matthew XXIII—Criticism, interpretation, etc. 2. Heretics, Christian. 3. Cults—Controversial literature. I. Title. II. Series:
MacArthur, John F. Bible studies.
BS2575.M24   1986   226'.206   86-23505
ISBN 0-8024-5345-7

1 2 3 4 5 6 Printing / GB / Year 91 90 89 88 87 86

Printed in the United States of America

Contents

CHAPTER   PAGE

1. The Character of False Spiritual Leaders—Part 1   7
   Tape GC 2360—Matthew 23:1-4

2. The Character of False Spiritual Leaders—Part 2   29
   Tape GC 2361—Matthew 23:5-12

3. The Condemnation of False Spiritual Leaders—Part 1   45
   Tape GC 2362—Matthew 23:13, 15

4. The Condemnation of False Spiritual Leaders—Part 2   63
   Tape GC 2363—Matthew 23:16-33

5. Jesus' Last Words to Israel—Part 1   83
   Tape GC 2364—Matthew 23:34-36

6. Jesus' Last Words to Israel—Part 2   101
   Tape GC 2365—Matthew 23:37-39

   Scripture Index   121

These Bible studies are taken from messages delivered by Pastor-Teacher John MacArthur, Jr., at Grace Community Church in Panorama City, California. These messages have been combined into a 6-tape album entitled *Exposing False Spiritual Leaders*. You may purchase this series either in an attractive vinyl cassette album or as individual cassettes. To purchase these tapes, request the album *Exposing False Spiritual Leaders*, or ask for the tapes by their individual GC numbers. Please consult the current price list; then, send your order, making your check payable to:

WORD OF GRACE COMMUNICATIONS
P.O. Box 4000
Panorama City, CA 91412

Or call the following number:
818-982-7000

1

The Character of False Spiritual Leaders— Part 1

Outline

Introduction

Lesson
I. The Discussion About False Spiritual Leaders (v. 1)
  A. The Setting
    1. The interaction with the false spiritual leaders
    2. The indictment of the false spiritual leaders
  B. The Subjects
    1. The identity of the scribes and Pharisees
    2. The origin of the scribes and Pharisees
II. The Description of False Spiritual Leaders (vv. 2-7)
  A. They Lack Authority (v. 2)
    1. The seat of authority
    2. The stealing of authority
      a) The correspondence
        (1) Jeremiah 14
        (2) Jeremiah 23
        (3) Isaiah 30
        (4) John 10
      b) The contrast
  B. They Lack Integrity (v. 3)
    1. The Pharisees' words were correct
    2. The Pharisees' works were condemned
      a) Because they lacked spiritual power
      b) Because Scripture condemned them

      (1) Matthew 23
      (2) 2 Peter 2
      (3) Jude
    c) Because their consciences were seared
C. They Lack Sympathy (v. 4)
  1. The picture
  2. The pile
  3. The passages
  4. The perversion

Conclusion

Introduction

There have always been and will always be false spiritual leaders who pretend to represent God. The Old Testament warns people to stay away from them. Moses encountered them in Egypt, and Jeremiah fought with them in Judah. Ezekiel faced them and called them foolish prophets who followed their own spirit and saw nothing (Ezek. 13:3). In the New Testament, our Lord describes them as false Christs and false prophets who will show great signs and wonders (Matt. 24:24). Paul refers to them as preachers of another gospel in Galatians 1:8-9. In 1 Timothy 4:1 he calls them purveyors of the doctrines of demons. Peter said they were false preachers who secretly bring in damnable heresies, like dogs who return to lick up their own vomit (2 Pet. 2:1, 22). The apostle John saw many antichrists already present who denied that Jesus was the true Christ (1 John 2:18, 22). Jude called them dreamers who defile the flesh (Jude 8). Paul summed it up well when he said that false spiritual leaders are wolves whose desire is to enter in, not sparing the flock (Acts 20:29).

Passages of Scripture that look to the future time tell us that shortly before the second coming of Jesus Christ false prophets will proliferate. Yet false prophets were also hard at work in Palestine during the time of Jesus. At His first coming, all hell massed its forces for a three-year assault on Christ and His truth. Therefore, false spiritual leaders are mentioned often in the gospel record. In Matthew 23 the Lord Jesus Christ confronts them with a denunciation that blisters and burns as it comes from His lips, and only in the last three verses of the chapter are there words of tenderness and pity.

Lesson

I. THE DISCUSSION ABOUT FALSE SPIRITUAL LEADERS (v. 1)

"Then spoke Jesus to the multitude, and to his disciples."

Matthew 23 can be divided into three sections. In the first twelve verses Jesus speaks to the crowd and the disciples, and then from verses 13 to 36 He speaks to the scribes and Pharisees. Finally, the chapter closes with a moment of tender compassion over the plight of Israel.

A. The Setting

1. The interaction with the false spiritual leaders

The setting of the first twelve verses is the Wednesday of Passion Week. In the morning the Lord came into Jerusalem from Bethany, where He had spent the night, possibly with Lazarus, Mary, and Martha. On the way to Jerusalem, Jesus cursed a fig tree and taught His disciples a lesson (Matt. 21:18-22). Arriving at the Temple, which He had cleansed the day before, He began to teach. As He was teaching the multitudes visiting Jerusalem for the Passover, He was stopped by the religious leaders, who began dialoguing with Him (Matt. 21:23—23:39). They wanted to know by what authority He spoke. Jesus didn't give them an answer at first but instead gave them three parables that condemned them and told them they would be shut out of the kingdom of God and replaced by others.

The Jewish religious leaders then countered those parables of condemnation with three questions meant to discredit Him, each of which He answered in a way that discredited them. Finally, He asked them a question about the Messiah, which proved beyond a shadow of a

9

doubt that the Messiah was both man and God. Then they stopped asking Him questions.

2. The indictment of the false spiritual leaders

As we begin verse 1 of chapter 23, the dialogue has ended, and the Lord gives His last sermon to the people of Israel; His ministry to them is over. This final public speech is a denunciation of false religious leaders and a warning for the people to stay away from them. It is a severe condemnation, but a necessary one, since the Pharisees were false shepherds. They were wolves in sheeps' clothing.

This was not the first time Christ had denounced false spiritual leaders. A few months before, as recorded in Luke 11:39-54, He said things that were similar to what He was saying now. He had already confronted them and called them what they truly were, but now He warned the people to stay away from them.

The Lord knew that He would die on Friday. He knew that soon after that He would ascend to heaven, and the work He had started would be left with His disciples. It was essential that the people be warned to stay away from false religious leaders and follow the true spiritual leaders. Christ knew that His disciples, the true spiritual leaders, would soon be filled with the Spirit of God and go everywhere preaching the gospel. He wanted the people to be ready to listen to them. He was setting up His disciples for their ministry, which is why in verses 8-12 He calls His disciples to be different from the false spiritual leaders. Jesus' message wasn't just a denunciation of the leaders; it was also a warning to the people.

We know Christ succeeded in directing many people away from the false spiritual leaders to His disciples because on the first day the disciples preached, the Day of Pentecost, three thousand people believed and were baptized (Acts 2). Shortly after that, thousands more believed. By the events recorded in Acts 4, there were as many as twenty thousand who heard and believed in the apostolic preaching. In Acts 5:28 the Jewish leaders complain that those preachers had filled all Jerusalem with their teaching.

B. The Subjects

In verse 1 Jesus addresses the multitude and His disciples, but that doesn't mean the scribes and Pharisees do not hear. We know they must have heard, because they had been there for the whole questioning process in chapter 22. And in verse 13 when Christ directs His words directly to these false leaders, the rest of the crowd hear as well. This electrifying scene helps us understand why the false leaders had to get rid of Jesus; the Lord's blistering public denunciation threatened their own credibility and careers.

In verse 2 Jesus mentions the scribes and the Pharisees, who were the subjects of His remarks. Not all of them were equally deserving of this rebuke. There might have been some who had some integrity, like Paul, a Pharisee who acted ignorantly out of unbelief. For the most part, however, the words of our Lord fit both groups.

1. The identity of the scribes and Pharisees

There were various sects in Judaism, the dominant one being the Pharisees, who were the religious leaders. The Sadducees, another sect, were primarily interested in politics and amassing fortunes. They weren't really involved in theology and spiritual leadership, though they had some positions of authority in the hierarchy of the Temple. Another group, the Zealots, were political nationalists. The Essenes were a group of monastic people who never really had an impact on society because they separated themselves from it. Finally, there were the Herodians, a political party that favored the Herods (the political rulers appointed by Rome). The bulk of spiritual leadership fell to the Pharisees, who may have numbered no more than six thousand. They were highly influential and committed to the law.

2. The origin of the scribes and Pharisees

In 586 B.C. the people of Judah were taken into captivity to Babylon for seventy years. Following that period of captivity, they came back from Babylon and started to reestablish life in the land of Israel. Nehemiah and Ezra brought the Scripture to the people again, and, as recounted in Nehemiah 8, there was a public reading. The people all stood and swore to obey the Scriptures and be committed to God's authority. The law was put back in the center of national life, and the people were committed to it.

At that time a group of people became committed to studying and teaching the Scriptures. From the time of the reading of Nehemiah chapter 8, down to the time of our Lord, that group had studied the law and interpreted it to the point where they had more than fifty volumes of commentary on the law. They added all kinds of ceremonies, rituals, and regulations, and they forced them on the people. For them, life was all about the law.

Among the Pharisees were the scribes, who were the experts in the law. All Pharisees were committed to keeping the law, but the scribes were especially devoted to the law and were teachers of the law. An old Jewish saying said that God gave the law to Moses, Moses gave the law to Joshua, Joshua gave the law to the elders, the elders gave the law to the prophets, and the prophets gave the law to the men of the synagogues (the scribes). So they were the spiritual leaders, and they considered themselves to be the guardians of the law.

A Pharisee Sampler

William Barclay, who spent part of his life in the land of Israel researching the cultural background of the New Testament, noted that the Talmud speaks of seven kinds of Pharisees (*Sotah* 22*b*). He gave them the following titles:

1. The "shoulder" Pharisee

The "shoulder" Pharisee wore his good deeds on his shoulders: he paraded the good he did. When he prayed, he would put ashes on his head, and he would look sad so everyone would know how pious and spiritual he was.

2. The "wait a little" Pharisee

The "wait a little" Pharisee could always come up with a spiritual reason to put off doing something good. He always had excuses that sounded pious.

3. The "bruised and bleeding" Pharisee

The "bruised and bleeding" Pharisee thought it was a sin to look at a woman, so whenever women were around, he bent over and closed his eyes. He kept running into walls as a result. According to the Pharisees, the more bruises you had, the more holy you were.

4. The "humpback tumbling" Pharisee

The "humpback tumbling" Pharisee desired to show his humility, so he slouched over, bent his back, and walked around all day in that humble position. He also thought it was wrong to lift his feet, so he shuffled them. Consequently, he kept tripping on things and tumbling.

5. The "ever reckoning" Pharisee

The "ever reckoning" Pharisee kept count of all his good deeds so he'd know what God owed him in terms of blessing.

6. The "fearing" Pharisee

Fear of being sent to hell motivated all the things the "fearing" Pharisee did.

7. The "God fearing" Pharisee

The "God fearing" Pharisee did what he did he out of proper motives, and he had integrity. He was the only one out the seven who was good.

II. THE DESCRIPTION OF FALSE SPIRITUAL LEADERS
   (vv. 2-7)

The Lord points out in verses 2-7 five qualities that a false spiritual leader lacks: authority, integrity, sympathy, spirituality, and humility. Those are also things that all true spiritual leaders possess.

This is a description of false spiritual leaders in first-century Palestine, but the principles our Lord expresses here can apply to our time as well. They are truly the marks of all false spiritual leaders, and they're important for us to know so we can identify them in our day.

A. They Lack Authority (v. 2)

"The scribes and the Pharisees sit in Moses' seat."

1. The seat of authority

   In the synagogues there was a special seat called Moses' seat. That seat (which may not have been a real chair) stood for a place of authority. Just as our modern universities have a "chair of philosophy," a "chair of history," or a "chair of biology," so the synagogue had the chair of Moses. It was held by the leading teacher, the leading Pharisee, or the leading scribe. If you held the seat of Moses in your synagogue, you would be the chief teacher of that synagogue. The word *seat* is the Greek word *kathedra* from which we get the word *cathedral*. The Romans took the word *kathedra* and made a phrase out of it: *ex cathedra*, "out of the place of authority." It is said in the Roman Catholic church that when the Pope speaks *ex cathedra*, his teaching is binding on one's conscience and life. *Kathedra* had to do with authority, and Moses had to do with the law, so the scribes and Pharisees spoke as the authorities on the law.

2. The stealing of authority

   There is nothing in verse 2 to indicate that they had a right to sit in Moses' seat, telling the people what they should do as God's representatives. Nowhere do we read that they had earned such authority, that it had been given them by God, or that they were qualified to take it. All the text says is that they sat in Moses' seat.

The religious leaders did everything they could to try to keep Jesus from taking their authority from them. When He did go into their synagogues and teach, they were infuriated, just as they were when Paul taught. In John 16, Jesus tells His disciples that the day would come when men would think they were doing service to God by throwing true believers out of their synagogues and killing them. A teacher who has real authority is always a threat to someone who is a usurper. These usurpers had occupied the chair of authority, when in fact they did not teach divine truth. They instead taught traditions, rituals, and routines that they themselves invented.

a) The correspondence

Other usurpers are mentioned in Scripture:

(1) Jeremiah 14

In Jeremiah's day, false spiritual leaders had usurped authority. Jeremiah was a true prophet but a lonely one. He was always telling the truth, but all the other prophets were lying. They were saying, "All will be well; everything is fine." Jeremiah was saying it wasn't, and the people would go to the teachers who said what they wanted to hear. The usurpers are condemned in Jeremiah 14:14: "The Lord said unto me, The prophets prophesy lies in my name." It is a fearful thing to propagate lies in the name of God. The verse continues, "I sent them not, neither have I commanded them, neither spoke unto them; they prophesy unto you a false vision and divination, and a thing of nought, and the deceit of their heart." God then went on to describe what He was going to do to those false spiritual leaders in the verses that follow.

15

(2) Jeremiah 23

In this chapter, false spiritual leaders are condemned again. God says in verse 21, "I have not sent these prophets, yet they ran; I have not spoken to them, yet they prophesied." Verse 32 says, "I am against those who prophesy false dreams, saith the Lord, and do tell them, and cause my people to err by their lies, and by their instability; yet I sent them not, nor commanded them." (The same thought can be found in 27:15, 28:15, and 29:9.)

(3) Isaiah 30

The people of Isaiah's day were so used to false prophets that they rejected the true ones. In 30:10, we read that the people said, "Prophesy not unto us right things; speak unto us smooth things, prophesy deceits; get out of the way, turn aside out of the path, cause the Holy One of Israel to cease from before us." They wanted the true prophets to speak like the false ones they were accustomed to. That's an amazing thing. One of the reasons people go into false religions is they don't want to hear the truth, so there's always an audience for false prophets.

(4) John 10

In John 10:1-2 Jesus says that the true shepherd enters the sheepfold through the door, while those who climb into the sheepfold and don't come through the door are thieves and robbers. They have come to steal your life. False religious leaders are without authority. They don't speak for God and are not sent by God. They usurp authority and put demands on people, telling them things in the name of God that are not true.

b) The contrast

In contrast to the false spiritual leaders are those sent by the Lord. Like Paul, they have been made

16

ministers of the gospel, which is committed unto them (1 Cor. 9:17). Like Timothy, they have been called by God and set apart by the laying on of hands as confirmation (1 Tim. 4:14). They are like the apostles, on whom the Lord Jesus breathed and said, "Receive ye the Holy Spirit" (John 20:22), and to whom He said, "Go into all the world and preach the gospel" (Mark 16:15).

We see that false spiritual leaders lack authority. They take self-appointed seats of authority and fill them with their own ideas, traditions, and regulations, obscuring the law of God. When anyone threatens their authority, they become instantly hostile. There are multitudes of liars promoting falsehood and making up supposed visions. While claiming to represent God and speak in His name, they utter lies that lead men the world over into eternal damnation. There's only one authority, and that's the Word of God. Those who deviate from it are usurpers, as were the false leaders Jesus rebuked.

B. They Lack Integrity (v. 3)

"All, therefore, whatever they bid you observe, that observe and do; but do not after their works; for they say, and do not."

The false religious leaders' lack of authority made them usurpers, but their lack of integrity made them hypocrites.

1. The Pharisees' words were correct

How comprehensive is the word *all?* Obviously it can't be a comprehensive command to obey everything the Pharisees and scribes say because this whole discourse of our Lord tells us otherwise. In Matthew 5:21-48, the Lord sets His own authoritative teaching against the traditions of the rabbis. He tells them they are wrong about murder, divorce, adultery, and swearing. In chapter 6 He condemns their prayer habits, their practice of giving alms, and their worship. In chapter 15 He indicts them for having substituted the traditions of men for the commandments of God.

Since our Lord had already condemned much of the teaching of the scribes and Pharisees, He couldn't be saying here that the people were to obey everything they told them to do. The key to understanding His words is found in verse 2: "They sit in Moses' seat." Jesus was saying that whenever the scribes and Pharisees taught the law of Moses correctly, the people were to obey them.

Jesus wanted to avoid giving the impression that in condemning the false leaders, He was condemning their whole message. The people might then have thrown out the baby with the bath water. God's Word is God's Word, even in the mouth of a false teacher. When the Pharisees read the Word of God, it was binding on the hearts of the people. When they said to love and worship God, to love one's fellow man, and to love righteousness and hate evil, the people were to obey.

Jesus said to the crowd, "Observe and do." "Observe" (Gk., *tereō*) is in the present tense, and it means here "to keep observing." "Do" (Gk., *poieō*) is in the aorist tense, and it means here "to instantly respond." Our Lord was calling the people to an instant and continuous obedience to the law of God, no matter who taught it. Even in the mouth of a false prophet God's Word is still God's Word. Just as a clock that doesn't run is still correct twice a day, so false prophets occasionally will speak the truth.

2. The Pharisees' works were condemned

At the end of verse 3 Jesus says, "Do not after their works." Why? "For they say, and do not." They were hypocrites. The people were to obey the Word of God when the scribes and Pharisees taught it correctly, but they were not to follow their example, because they didn't practice what they taught. They were phonies who lacked integrity.

a) Because they lacked spiritual power

The scribes and Pharisees couldn't live out the requirements of the law, because unsaved people have no internal ability to restrain evil and do good. They could be outwardly moral and outwardly ethical and could develop sophisticated ethics and morality. They could talk about God, about loving everyone, and doing good to the poor. They could be strong on the family, and all that is commendable. But they weren't able to do what they asked the people to do. It is only through redemption that a person receives a new nature. Ephesians 2:10 says that a redeemed person should lead a life that exudes good works. Paul says in Romans 7:22, following his redemption, "I delight in the law of God after the inward man." Unredeemed people, no matter what their ethics are, have no internal power to restrain their evil or promote good because they have an unredeemed, sinful nature.

b) Because Scripture condemned them

(1) Matthew 23

In verse 23 Jesus says that the Pharisees give a tithe of mint (a tiny herb), anise (a small plant), and cumin (a little seed) but that they omit the weightier matters of the law, like justice, mercy, and faith. Why? Because they were incapable of producing those things on their own.

In verse 25 Jesus says that they clean the outside of the cup and the platter but are full of extortion and excess within. In verse 27 He says they are like whited tombs in that they appear beautiful on the outside but inside are full of dead men's bones and all uncleanness. In verse 33 He calls them snakes and says they are damned to hell. Verse 28 summarizes the Lord's rebuke of these false leaders: outwardly they appear righteous, but inwardly they are full of hypocrisy and lawlessness.

(2) 2 Peter 2

This chapter is a description of false spiritual leaders in vivid and almost shocking terms. In verse 1 we read, "There were false prophets also among the people, even as there shall be false teachers among you, who secretly shall bring in destructive heresies." In verse 10 Peter says that they walk after the flesh in the lust of uncleanness, they despise authority, and are presumptuous and self-willed. Verse 12 says they are brute beasts who speak evil of things they don't understand and will utterly perish in their own corruption. Verse 13 calls them scabs and spots that revel in their own deceptions. Verse 14 says they're sexually unrestrained, even though they may not appear that way outwardly. Verse 15 says they are cursed children who have forsaken the right way. Verse 17 says they are "wells without water, clouds that are carried with a tempest, to whom the mist of darkness is reserved forever." They are corrupt to the very core (v. 19).

(3) Jude

Jude referred to false spiritual leaders in much the same terminology as Peter. He calls them filthy dreamers who defile the flesh and despise authority in verse 8. In verse 10 he calls them brute beasts that corrupt themselves. In verses 12 and 13 they are called clouds without water; trees with withered fruit, twice dead, plucked up by the roots; raging waves of the sea foaming out their own shame; and wandering stars to whom is reserved the blackness of darkness forever.

That is how Scripture characterizes a false spiritual leader. He tries the best he can to restrain his vice, but it fills him. Since he has no spiritual capacity to restrain evil, it manifests itself in his life.

c) Because their consciences were seared

Paul characterized false spiritual leaders as "speaking lies in hypocrisy, having their conscience seared with a hot iron" (1 Tim. 4:2). That is a vivid phrase. Their consciences became like scar tissue. Paul was saying that their consciences have become so cal-

20

loused that they are no longer sensitive to the hypocritical nature of their existence. They are liars who have lied so long, hypocrites who have lived hypocritically so long, that they are desensitized to it.

False spiritual leaders aren't nice people who have a moral approach to life and who just happen not to know Christ. They set an external standard that they can't live up to. Vice is not restrained nor is righteousness promoted in an unregenerate, fallen heart. If you examine any of the religious systems that don't adhere to the Bible or that add to it, you will find people advocating ethical and moral standards that they themselves can't keep. They lack the power to restrain the evil in their lives; consequently there's an utter absence of true righteousness in them.

The world shouldn't be shocked by false spiritual leaders such as Jim Jones. He appeared to be so ethical and concerned for the poor, but his evil manifested itself by the mass suicide of himself and his followers. However, the wickedness of false spiritual leaders doesn't always come out that dramatically, and in some cases it won't be apparent until the final judgment.

C. They Lack Sympathy (v. 4)

"For they bind heavy burdens and grievous to be borne, and lay them on men's shoulders, but they themselves will not move them with one of their fingers."

The third thing the Lord condemns the false spiritual leaders for is their lack of sympathy. They were not only usurpers and hypocrites, but they were also loveless.

1. The picture

The picture in verse 4 is of a man loading up his donkey. You would be surprised what they put on their donkeys in the Middle East. They pile things so high on top and down over the sides that sometimes you can hardly see the animal. We saw boxes piled ten to fifteen feet high, and once I saw a donkey with chickens in little crates hanging all over it. While the donkey labors under its huge load, the man walks alongside carrying nothing.

He wouldn't even straighten the load if the donkey started to list. That would have been a vivid picture to the people of Jesus' day.

2. The pile

The scribes and Pharisees piled on regulations and rules and rituals and traditions until the load was impossible to carry. On top of that was the guilt of failure. The biggest burden of all was their works-righteousness system, which said that if your good deeds outweighed your bad, you'd get to heaven, but if your bad deeds outweighed your good, you'd go to hell. There was no way to get rid of the bad pile; it just stayed there, and you had to keep on trying to balance it with good deeds. That placed an intolerable burden on the people.

Religion for them was a depressing, impossible life of continual demands, with no hope of relief. The false religious leaders never came along with the finger of grace to remove the burden. But Jesus completely removes the bad pile at salvation.

3. The passages

a) Galatians 1, 5

When the apostle Paul preached the gospel in Galatia, he preached the message of grace, forgiveness, and mercy. He was followed by false religious leaders who told the Galatians that they had to keep the law of Moses and all the traditions to be saved. Paul was so upset that he said they should be damned for saying that (Gal. 1:8-9). In chapter 5 he says, "Stand fast, therefore, in the liberty with which Christ hath made us free, and be not entangled again with the yoke of bondage" (v. 1).

b) 1 Peter 5:7

The Pharisees, with all their religious rituals, were not interested in talking about grace, forgiveness, and mercy. They saddled the people with external moral standards and then left them to live under the guilt of not being able to measure up. The Pharisees showed no sympathy, no love, no tenderness, no caring. They did nothing to help to shoulder the people's burdens.

The sentiment behind 1 Peter 5:7, "[Cast] all your care upon him; for he careth for you," would have been foreign to them. They didn't know the tender Shepherd who carries the little ones in His own arms.

c) Mark 12:40

In Mark 12:40, which is a parallel passage to Matthew 23, the Lord says it is typical of the scribes and Pharisees to devour widows' houses. They moved in on the widow who couldn't pay the rent and made her destitute. They abused and grieved people.

d) 1 Timothy 4:3

Paul says in this verse that false spiritual leaders would come around forbidding people to marry. What a ridiculous thing! That is a far cry from what the Lord intended when He said through the apostle Peter that marriage is the grace of life (1 Pet. 3:7). Paul went on to say that the false leaders would make people abstain from certain kind of foods. How foolish! God has given us all things to be received with thanksgiving (1 Tim. 4:4).

e) 2 Peter 2:3

Peter said that the false leaders make merchandise out of people. They just use and abuse you; you're part of the building of their empire. You're part of what feeds their spiritual egos.

f) Isaiah 10:1-2

An unsympathetic attitude on the part of false spiritual leaders is not new. Isaiah said, "Woe unto them who decree unrighteous decrees . . . to turn aside the needy from justice and to take away the right from the poor . . . that widows may be their prey, and that they may rob the fatherless!" The religious leaders were fleecing the sheep instead of feeding the sheep.

g) Jeremiah 7:4-7

God says in this passage, "Trust not in lying words, saying, The temple of the Lord, The temple of the Lord, The temple of the Lord" (v. 4). In other words, the false prophets were saying that their teaching was God's truth. He goes on to say in verses 5-7, "If ye thoroughly amend your ways and your doings; if ye thoroughly execute justice between a man and his neighbor; if ye oppress not the sojourner, the father- less, and the widow, and shed not innocent blood in this place, neither walk after other gods to your harm; then will I cause you to dwell in this place." God in effect says, "Don't give me all that pious talk; go out and be fair to a stranger, take care of an or- phan and a widow, and stop devouring those people for your own ends."

h) Ezekiel 34:1-9

In the thirty-fourth chapter of Ezekiel, God indicts the false shepherds of Israel. Ezekiel wrote, "The word of the Lord came unto me saying, Son of Man, prophesy against the shepherds of Israel; prophesy, and say unto them, Thus saith the Lord God unto the shepherds: Woe be to the shepherds of Israel that do feed themselves! Should not the shepherds feed the flocks?" (vv. 1-2).

Spiritual leaders are often criticized because they de- vour people. They build great empires, amass great fortunes, and build great names for themselves—all at the expense of poor, unwitting people. Only God knows how many people have been bilked by reli- gious charlatans. Verse 3 says, "Ye eat the fat, and ye clothe yourselves with the wool." They were feeding on their own sheep. Instead of reaching out to meet their needs, they were devouring them, taking every- thing they had. Ezekiel goes on to say, "Ye kill

24

those who are fed, but ye feed not the flock. The diseased have ye not strengthened, neither have ye healed that which was sick, neither have ye bound up that which was broken, neither have ye brought again that which was driven away, neither have ye sought that which was lost, but with force and cruelty have ye ruled them" (vv. 3-4).

That is such an accurate definition of false religious leaders. They brutalize people, taking everything they can get out of them to build their empire. Verses 5-9 say, "They were scattered, because there is no shepherd; and they became food to all the beasts of the field when they were scattered. My sheep wandered through all the mountains, and upon every high hill; yea, my flock was scattered upon all the face of the earth, and none did search or seek after them. Therefore ye shepherds, hear the word of the Lord. As I live, saith the Lord God, surely, because my flock became a prey, and my flock became food to every beast of the field, because there was no shepherd, neither did my shepherds search for my flock, but the shepherds fed themselves, and fed not my flock, Therefore, O ye shepherds, hear the word of the Lord. . . . I am against the shepherds."

4. The perversion

Jesus looked out over the multitude and saw them as sheep without shepherds (Matt. 9:36). There wasn't anyone to feed them, to pick them up and carry them, to bind up their wounds, or to restore them. There wasn't anyone to lift a finger to ease their load. The Pharisees wouldn't remove their burdens. The word translated "move" in Matthew 23:4 could better be translated "remove," as the same term in Revelation 6:14 has that sense. They wouldn't remove that burden at all by preaching a message of grace. They wouldn't act out of love. It must have been a wonderful moment for those who heard Jesus say, "Come unto me all ye that labor and are heavy laden, and I will give you rest. Take my yoke and learn of me; for I am meek and lowly in heart and ye shall find rest unto your souls. For my yoke is easy, and my burden is light" (Matt. 11:28-30). Jesus'

25

words stand in contrast to the heavy burdens that the false spiritual leaders put on the people.

In our day we also have false religious leaders who bind people with one demand after another: telling them whom they can marry, where they can live, or how many children they can have, for instance. They never offer a word of grace or forgiveness. They never show any tenderness or that they care about the needs of their people.

Conclusion

We've seen the first three characteristics of false spiritual leaders. They lack true authority, integrity, and sympathy. The true spiritual leader, however, has true authority, which he gets from his proper interpretation of Scripture. If we examine his life over a period of time, we can see that he has integrity because he practices what he preaches. Finally, he is sympathetic: The greatest desire of his heart is to feed his flock, not to fleece them. Rather than building his own empire, he is a good shepherd who gently carries those who are wounded.

Focusing on the Facts

1. What are some of the terms the Bible uses to describe false spiritual leaders (see p. 8)?
2. At which two periods of history will false leaders be most active (see p. 8)?
3. On what day of our Lord's Passion Week was His message given (see p. 9)?
4. To what two groups did Jesus address His remarks (see p. 10)?
5. Was this the first time Jesus had denounced false spiritual leaders? Justify your answer (see p. 10).
6. What was our Lord's purpose in giving this message (see p. 10)?
7. What was the dominant religious sect in Judaism (see p. 11)?

8. To what event did the scribes and Pharisees trace their origin (see p. 12)?

9. Explain what is meant by the "seat of Moses" (Matt. 23:2; see p. 14).

10. Who granted the scribes and Pharisees the right to sit in Moses' seat (see pp. 14-15)?

11. Was the usurping of authority by the scribes and Pharisees unique in biblical history (see pp. 15-16)?

12. Did Jesus mean for his hearers to obey everything that the scribes and Pharisees commanded them to do? Explain (see pp. 17-18).

13. What two things did Jesus command the people to do in response to the teaching of the scribes and Pharisees (Matt. 23:3; see p. 18)?

14. Why are false spiritual leaders unable to live out the principles they teach to others (see pp. 18-19)?

15. Why does the conscience of a false leader not condemn him for his hypocrisy (1 Tim. 4:2; see pp. 20-21)?

16. Describe the scribes and Pharisees' lack of sympathy (see pp. 21-22).

17. What do each of the following passages tell us about the character of a false spiritual leader: Mark 12:40; 1 Timothy 4:3; 2 Peter 2:3; Isaiah 10:1-2; and Ezekiel 34:1-9 (see pp. 23-25)?

18. What is the significance of Jesus' words in Matthew 11:28 (see pp. 25-26)?

19. What are three characteristics of the true spiritual leader that we can learn from this chapter (see p. 26)?

Pondering the Principles

1. One of the best ways to spot a counterfeit object is to become familiar with the genuine article. How familiar are you with the truths of the Christian faith? Do you have a basic understanding of the major doctrines of the Christian faith—the doctrines of God, Christ, Scripture, salvation, sanctification, angels, the church, and last things (eschatology)? Do you recognize false teaching when you hear it? Would you be comfortable defending what you believe if someone attacked it? Pick one area of Christian truth you are weak in, and begin studying it this week. Start your study by reading a book, listening to a tape, or even taking a correspondence course from a Bible college. If you

aren't sure what resources to use for your study, ask your pastor or visit a Christian bookstore.

2. One of the marks of a false spiritual leader is hypocrisy: he says one thing and does another. Christians can also be guilty of having their lives not match up with what they profess to believe. Spend some time alone with God examining your life. Do you practice what you believe in your personal life? What about in your marriage? On the job? At school? If you find some areas where you are falling short, confess that to God, and commit yourself to changing your attitudes and behavior. Seek to make yourself accountable to another person in the area in which you struggle.

2

The Character of False Spiritual Leaders— Part 2

Outline

Introduction
A. False Spiritual Leaders Are a Cause for Concern
B. False Spiritual Leaders Are Abundant
C. False Spiritual Leaders Are Dangerous

Review
 I. The Discussion About False Spiritual Leaders (vv. 1-2)
II. The Description of False Spiritual Leaders (vv. 3-7)
   A. They Lack Authority (v. 2)
   B. They Lack Integrity (v. 3)
   C. They Lack Sympathy (v. 4)

Lesson
D. They Lack Spirituality (v. 5)
   1. Their condemnation by others
      a) Jesus
         (1) Their giving
         (2) Their praying
         (3) Their fasting
      b) Jude
         (1) Their separation
         (2) Their sensuality

2. Their commendation of themselves
    a) In their phylacteries
        (1) The description of phylacteries
        (2) The derivation of phylacteries
        (3) The desecration of phylacteries
    b) In their garments
E. They Lack Humility (vv. 6-7)
    1. They seek the preeminent places (v. 6)
        a) At the feasts
        b) In the synagogues
    2. They seek the public praises (v. 7)
        a) In the title *Rabbi*
        b) In the title *Master*
        c) In the title *Father*
III. The Declaration to True Spiritual Leaders (vv. 8-12)
    A. Avoid Elevated Titles (vv. 8-10)
        1. Rabbi (v. 8)
        2. Father (v. 9)
        3. Master (v. 10)
    B. Accept Lowly Service (vv. 11-12)

Conclusion

Introduction

A. False Spiritual Leaders Are a Cause for Concern

One of the duties of a pastor is to warn his people. The apostle Paul told the Ephesian elders that he had spent years warning them about false spiritual leaders who would try to take them away from the truth (Acts 20:29-31). Paul was not the first to warn his people, for true spiritual leaders have always been called to a ministry of warning because the world is filled with false spiritual leadership.

B. False Spiritual Leaders Are Abundant

You can see the advertisements of false spiritual leaders in the church page of the Saturday paper. They occupy places of authority in the false religions of the world, the cults, and the occult, and they have even found their way into Christianity. They masquerade as those who represent God, but they do not. The sad fact is they lead the souls of men and women to hell while promising them heaven.

C. False Spiritual Leaders Are Dangerous

In Matthew 23:15 our Lord says to the false spiritual leaders of His day, "Ye compass sea and land to make one proselyte [convert], and when he is made, ye make him twofold more the child of hell than yourselves." False spiritual leadership has to be confronted with great seriousness, for it leads the souls of men into condemnation while giving them the illusion that they have found God and are pleasing to Him. That is why false spiritual leaders receive the greatest condemnation of anyone in Scripture. And Matthew 23 contains the strongest condemnation of them in the Bible.

Matthew 23 can be divided into several parts. It begins with a call to the people to avoid false teachers and is followed by a condemnation of the teachers themselves. It closes with a lament over the people who will be judged for following their teaching. Jesus says things here that are difficult to hear and sometimes painful—but still necessary.

Review

I. THE DISCUSSION ABOUT FALSE SPIRITUAL LEADERS (vv. 1-2; see pp. 9-13)

II. THE DESCRIPTION OF FALSE SPIRITUAL LEADERS (vv. 3-7; see pp. 14-26)

A. They Lack Authority (v. 2; see pp. 14-17)

B. They Lack Integrity (v. 3; see pp. 17-21)

C. They Lack Sympathy (v. 4; see pp. 21-26)

D. They Lack Spirituality (v. 5)

The religion of the scribes and Pharisees was all outward show for the purpose of satisfying their fleshly desires. They wanted to seem pious so they could get the homage and reverence of the people. As it says at the end of Galatians, they desired to make "a fair show in the flesh" (6:12). And as our Lord says here in verse 5, "But all their works they do to be seen of men."

1. Their condemnation by others

   a) Jesus

   In Matthew 6 the Lord rebukes their false religion.

   (1) Their giving

   Jesus says in verse 1, "Take heed that ye do not your alms before men, to be seen by them." He goes on to say in verse 2 that when you do give alms, not to sound a trumpet before you. The Temple's courtyard of the women had receptacles on the walls for the offerings. When the Pharisees went in, they would have a fanfare sounded on a trumpet to announce their arrival. They wanted everyone to watch them give and think they were devout. Jesus condemned the giving of the scribes and Pharisees as mere outward show.

   (2) Their praying

   In verse 5 Jesus condemns their manner of praying. He called them hypocrites who love to pray standing in the middle of the synagogue and in the crossroads of the streets. They would pray their daily prayers in public places, so that everyone would see how pious they were.

(3) Their fasting

> When the scribes and Pharisees fasted, they
> would put ashes on their faces to make them look
> pale so that everyone would think they were de-
> vout. Jesus warned the people not to be like that
> (vv. 10-18).

b) Jude

(1) Their separation

> Verse 19 of the epistle of Jude describes false spir-
> itual leaders as "they who separate themselves."
> They wanted to be considered a spiritual elite
> and often dressed differently to appear pious. (In-
> cidentally, the word *Pharisee* may come from a
> word that means "separated.") The scribes and
> Pharisees thought of themselves as better than
> everyone else and expected to be revered. Their
> sole objective was to be seen by men, so Jesus
> says in Matthew 6, "They have their
> reward"—that is, they are seen by men. As a re-
> sult, however, they will receive no reward from
> God. Instead they will receive judgment.

(2) Their sensuality

> Jude 19 also says that false spiritual leaders are
> sensual. The word translated "sensual" is a form
> of the Greek word *psuchikos*, which has to do
> with the physical part of life as opposed to the
> spiritual dimension, and is often translated
> "soul." False spiritual leaders are not in tune
> with the spiritual realities of life; they don't con-
> sider that which is at the core of man's being. All
> they think about is the physical; they are void of
> any spiritual sense. In fact, verse 19 goes on to
> say that false teachers do not possess the Spirit.

False spiritual leaders deceive millions into thinking
that they represent God. They head religious organi-

zations, seminaries, and colleges. They even pastor churches and teach, but all their efforts are for the gratification of their earthly appetites, which comes from being thought of as pious and devout. Religion for them is little more than a means of building up their egos.

2. Their commendation of themselves

In verse 5 the Lord identifies two ways in which the scribes and Pharisees commend themselves to men. He says, "They make broad their phylacteries and enlarge the borders of their garments." Their religion emphasized that which was visible, in contrast to 1 Corinthians chapter 4, which teaches that all who serve Christ will ultimately be judged regarding the motives of the heart.

a) In their phylacteries

(1) The description of phylacteries

The word *phylactery* can be defined as "a means of protection." A phylactery was a charm, or an amulet. The Egyptians and other pagan peoples around Israel wore charms to ward off evil spirits, and as the Jews drifted away from God toward pagan expressions of religion, they also wanted charms, so they developed phylacteries. They made them square and covered them with black leather from a ceremonially clean animal. They then connected leather straps to them with twelve stitches each, one stitch for each of the twelve tribes of Israel. They used the leather straps to tie one phylactery on their forehead and another on their left hand. (They believed the left hand was closer to the heart.)

The box contained four sections of the Mosaic law: Exodus 13:1-10, Exodus 13:11-16, Deuteronomy 6:4-9, and Deuteronomy 11:13-21. One box contained all of those verses written on one piece of parchment, while the other box contained each verse written on separate pieces of parchment.

They then strapped one of the boxes to the head and the other to the hand. To demonstrate the extent to which this whole magical approach to religion had gone, the Talmud implies that the phylacteries were more sacred than the gold plate on the forehead of the high priest because the gold plate had the name of God on it only once, but the phylacteries contained the name of God several times (*Shabbath* 12*a*). They taught that God Himself wore phylacteries all the time, since the Pharisees thought of God as a glorified rabbi, who studied the law three hours a day.

On the little box was written the Hebrew letter *shin*. When a man tied the straps of the box on the back of his head, he made a knot in the form of another Hebrew letter, the *daleth*. When he strapped the box onto his hand, he wound the strap seven times around the arm and three times around the hand, creating the Hebrew letter *yodh*. By the time he was finished putting on the phylacteries, he was wearing the consonants that form the Hebrew word *Shaddai*, which means "almighty." He thought he was creating a magical charm with God's name to ward off demons.

In Orthodox Judaism today, a boy gets his set of phylacteries when he's thirteen years old, and he wears them at the designated times of prayer. In our day, as in the time of Christ, women do not wear phylacteries. The usual custom was to wear them during prayer, but the Pharisees wore them all the time. Whenever they appear in the New Testament, they should be pictured as wearing those little boxes on their heads and left arms.

Flaming Phylacteries

The story is told in rabbinic literature of a rabbi who went to see a Gentile king. According to Jewish tradition, rabbis were superior to kings, so when he left, he turned his back to the king and walked out. That was a serious breach of custom, which demanded that persons leaving the presence of a king walk out backwards and bow as they went.

The king was so irate that he ordered his soldiers to kill the rabbi for his insulting behavior. As they moved toward the rabbi, the straps of his phylacteries began to blaze with fire, so the soldiers dared not touch him. That strange tale conveys some idea of how the Jewish people thought phylacteries provided magical protection.

(2) The derivation of phylacteries

In four places in the Old Testament (Ex. 13:9, 16; Deut. 6:8; 11:18), the Bible says that the commandments of God are to be upon the hand and between the eyes of God's people. That was a symbol of how the commandments of God are to be the controlling factor in what we think and what we do. Between the eyes speaks of the thought processes; on the hand symbolizes the activity of life.

The Jews at first interpreted those Old Testament commands as symbols of the fact that they were to give attention to God's Word in their thoughts and in their actions. Historically, there is no record of phylacteries until 400 B.C., which puts their origin in the intertestamental period. So they did not originate until relatively late in Israel's history, at a point when an external, legalistic approach to religion was being developed.

(3) The desecration of phylacteries

As the Jews became concerned with outward displays of piety, they began literally to put the law of God on their hands and on their heads. They were following the letter of their religion, but their hearts were far from God.

Not only did the Pharisees wear phylacteries, but verse 5 also says they made them large. They be-

36

lieved that one's devotion to God could be measured by the size of his phylacteries.

b) In their garments

According to verse 5, the scribes and Pharisees also enlarged the borders of their garments. In Numbers 15:37-41, God gives an interesting principle to the Jews. He said to add little tassels (Heb., *tallith*) to their clothing. The *tallith* was to mark them out as being set apart to God. That was commonly done; in fact Jesus wore them on His garment (Matt. 9:20). The Pharisees, however, made theirs bigger to show their devotion to God.

A little later in Jewish history, the *tallith* was worn on the inner garment instead of the outer. Today, Orthodox Jews wear them on their prayer shawls, and if you have ever seen one of those, you'll notice that it has a blue line in it and some blue fringe on it. That's the remnant of the *tallith*, and it marks them out as being Jewish.

The scribes and Pharisees wore boxes on their heads and had big fringes on their garments to prove they were utterly devoted to God. But it was all for show. Far from having true spirituality, they lacked it altogether.

E. They Lack Humility (vv. 6-7)

1. They seek the preeminent places (v. 6)

a) At the feasts

False spiritual leaders "love the uppermost places at feasts." The scribes and Pharisees sought the honor of sitting at the speaker's table, next to the host. The seats to the right and left of the host were the seats of honor. James and John knew that, which is why they sent their mother to ask Jesus if they could sit at His right and left in His kingdom (Matt. 20:20-21). False spiritual leaders love to be welcomed as if they are great and important people. When they attend a feast, they want to be recognized as the supreme guests of honor.

b) In the synagogues

In the synagogues, as in today's churches, there was a raised platform in the front. The scribes and Pharisees wanted to sit where everyone could see them. They wanted to sit with the dignitaries who prayed and read the Scriptures and thus parade their supposed piety before everyone. That's why I have such an aversion to sitting on a platform and why I sit in a pew before I preach. I'm just one of you who happens to have been called by God to teach, so when it's time to teach, I go up on the platform and do that. But I'm not going to elevate myself as if I were more devout or pious than everyone else.

The scribes and Pharisees were into religion for show, seeking prestige and honor from men. That's a sad thing. The church has some problems in this area, too. The chairs on some church platforms look like thrones. It makes me nervous to sit in those chairs. I'm not saying that everyone who sits in chairs on the platform has wrong motives. Sometimes pastors sit there because of tradition, and if I'm their guest, I'll sit up there, too. I sit at my share of speakers' tables, but I prefer not to.

2. They seek the public praises (v. 7)

When the scribes and Pharisees walked through the marketplace, they wanted to be recognized for who they were and greeted with the dignity that their office deserved. They had a lofty opinion of themselves. One pagan governor of Caesarea is portrayed in Jewish writings as rising up before rabbis because their faces looked to him like the faces of angels. Jewish writings contain elaborate directions about how they were supposed to be treated—and even lists of things to be done to people who didn't treat rabbis properly. They liked being called by formal titles; they wanted to be acknowledged as great people. In fact, one rabbi wrote that he wanted to be buried in white because he wanted the whole world to know how worthy he was to appear in the presence of God.

The story is told of a debate in heaven between the academy of rabbis and God. To solve the dispute, they had to get a decision from another rabbi. In the Talmud it is said that it is worse to act against the words of the scribes than against the words of Scripture (*Sanhedrin* 88*b*).

a) In the title *Rabbi*

The title *Rabbi* (v. 7) doesn't have the same connotation in our culture as it did in the Jewish culture of Jesus' day. It meant "teacher," but to say "teacher" in Jesus' day was to say, "supreme one, superior one, your excellency, most knowledgeable one, great one." The Latin equivalent is *docere*, which means "doctor." The scribes and Pharisees loved titles that elevated them above everyone else.

b) In the title *Master*

The word translated "Master" is the Greek word *kathēgētēs*, which is probably best translated "leader." The religious leaders loved to be called leader because that acknowledged them as the source of direction and guidance.

c) In the title *Father*

The scribes and Pharisees loved this title because they believed their teachings to be the source of spiritual life. Since they were the teachers, that would have made them the fathers of spiritual life.

III. THE DECLARATION TO TRUE SPIRITUAL LEADERS (vv. 8-12)

After rebuking the false spiritual leaders (the scribes and Pharisees) in verses 8-12, the Lord now tells the true spiritual leaders (His disciples) not to follow their example.

A. Avoid Elevated Titles (vv. 8-10)

1. Rabbi (v. 8)

Our Lord warned His disciples not to be called rabbi, since they had one teacher: Christ. That applies to me and all others who teach the Word of God. Christ is the teacher; we merely tell you what He said. We are not to elevate one person above another as if that person were the source of truth. The Lord tells us the reason at the end of verse 8: we are all brothers. No one is superior to anyone else; we're all on the same level.

We have tended to lose sight of that in the church. There is a place for honoring the teachers God has given us (1 Thess. 5:12-13; Heb. 13:7), but true spiritual leaders do not seek that. They seek to avoid anything that would elevate themselves at the expense of others.

2. Father (v. 9)

Jesus doesn't want us to call anyone Father, since no human being is the source of spiritual life. Some spiritual leaders in the church today want to be called Father, as if they were the source of spiritual life, but they are not. Verse 9 says there is only one Father and that He's in heaven.

3. Master (v. 10)

Jesus says in verse 10, "Neither be ye called masters [or leaders]: for one is your Master, even Christ." Christ is our Master, so we are not to appropriate for ourselves the title *Master*. None of us has insight into everything.

B. Accept Lowly Service (vv. 11-12)

In contrast to false spiritual leaders, Jesus tells His disciples in verse 11, "He that is greatest among you shall be your servant." Servants do not appropriate to themselves lofty titles, such as "Holy Reverend Doctor Bishop Slave" or "Right Reverend Father Master Guide Professor Footwasher"! True greatness consists in pouring out our lives for others. If you want to be great, then you must serve as Jesus served (Mark 9:35). Jesus humbled Himself by washing His disciples' feet, and He gave His life so others might live. Jesus said, "The Son of Man came not to be ministered unto, but to minister [serve], and to give his life" (Matt. 20:28). The greatest spiritual leader isn't the one with the most degrees or titles and the highest rank, but the one who gives the most to others.

Our Lord reinforces that truth in verse 12: "Whosoever shall exalt himself, shall be abased; and he that shall humble himself shall be exalted." If you want to be useful to the Lord, you must take the role of a servant, having no authority, knowledge, or wisdom apart from what God grants. When you see yourself simply as a servant, you understand where God wants you. Then in God's own time and God's own purpose, He will lift you up (James 4:10).

Peter learned that truth. In 1 Peter 5:2, he tells the elders: "Feed the flock of God which is among you, taking the oversight of it, not by constraint but willingly; not for filthy lucre but of a ready mind; neither as being lords over God's heritage." True spiritual leaders are not domineering. They are servants. Peter goes on to say in verse 5, "Be subject one to another, and be clothed with humility; for God resisteth the proud, and giveth grace to the humble." Self-exaltation has no place in those who represent Christ.

When Less Is More

Dr. Bonar was a dear man of God who lived many years ago. He once said he could always tell when a Christian was growing because a growing Christian would always talk more and more of Christ and less of himself. He said a growing Christian would see himself getting smaller and smaller until, like the morning star, he gave way to the rising sun.

Conclusion

The marks of a true spiritual leader are opposite from those that characterize a false one. A true spiritual leader possesses divine authority, which he obtains from the Word of God. He has integrity; His life matches his message. He does not lack sympathy but is filled with grace, mercy, pity, and concern. He possesses genuine spirituality, for his religion is not all for show. And he is humble, manifesting the heart of a servant.

Focusing on the Facts

1. Why are false spiritual leaders a cause for concern (see p. 30)?
2. Why are false spiritual leaders dangerous (see p. 31)?
3. In what areas was the lack of spirituality on the part of the scribes and Pharisees evident (see pp. 32-33)?
4. For what two things does Jude condemn false spiritual leaders (see p. 33)?
5. What is the primary motivating factor for the activities of false spiritual leaders (see p. 34)?
6. What were phylacteries (see pp. 34-35)?
7. Did the Jews wear phylacteries during the Old Testament period (see p. 36)?
8. Why did the Pharisees make their phylacteries large (see pp. 36-37)?
9. Since God commanded the Jewish people to wear fringes on their garments, why did Jesus condemn the scribes and Pharisees for wearing them (see p. 37)?
10. What does the behavior of the scribes and Pharisees at feasts and in the synagogues tell us about the genuineness of their religion (see pp. 37-38)?
11. Why did the scribes and Pharisees want to be called Rabbi (see p. 39)?
12. What was the significance of the title *Master* (see p. 39)?
13. Why did the scribes and Pharisees love the title *Father* (see p. 39)?
14. Explain why Jesus told His disciples not to be called Rabbi (see p. 40).
15. The disciples were not to call themselves Father because they were not the source of _____ (see p. 40).
16. What role should we seek if we want to become great (see pp. 40-41)?
17. What must we do to be useful to the Lord (see p. 41)?
18. Contrast the marks of a true spiritual leader with those of a false one (see pp. 41-42).

Pondering the Principles

1. Jesus denounced the false spiritual leaders of His day because they focused on the externals of religion. What do the following verses tell us about the type of worship God desires: 1 Samuel 16:7; Psalm 15; 51:6, 10; John 4:24; Romans 12:1-3; and James 1:27?

2. One of the crucial differences between a false spiritual leader and a true one is that the true spiritual leader is humble. What can we learn about humility from the examples of the following men: Abraham (Gen. 13:5-12); David (2 Sam. 7:18); Solomon (1 Kings 3:5-9); Isaiah (Isa. 6:5); Daniel (Dan. 2:30); John the Baptist (John 1:27; 3:30); the centurion (Luke 7:2-7); Paul (1 Cor. 15:9-10); and our Lord (Matt. 11:29)?

3

The Condemnation of False Spiritual Leaders—Part 1

Outline

Introduction
A. The Danger to Christianity
B. The Denunciation from Christ
   1. The subjects of the denunciation
   2. The specifics of the denunciation

Lesson
I. Explaining the Condemnation
   A. Its Two Main Characteristics
      1. The expression of wrath
      2. The expression of sorrow
   B. Its Two Main Components
      1. The word *woe*
      2. The word *hypocrite*
II. Expressing the Condemnation
   A. False Teachers Are Cursed for Their Exclusion (v. 13)
      1. The indictment of false spiritual leaders
      2. The intervention by false spiritual leaders
         a) The particulars
         b) The passages
   B. False Teachers Are Cursed for Their Perversion (v. 15)
      1. The propagation of false religion
         a) The scope of proselytization
         b) The security in proselytizing

2. The participants in false religion
    a) Those with cursory commitment
    b) Those with complete commitment
3. The product of false religion
    a) Described
    b) Depicted

Introduction

A. The Danger to Christianity

We hear much today about the threats of Communism, humanism, and secularism. We have to face the pressures of an immoral society every day. Many evangelical Christians are concerned about those threats, but all of those together do not pose as great a threat to Christianity as do false spiritual leaders. Without question, they have been and continue to be the most serious threat facing the church. In Matthew 23, we see that the Lord Jesus Christ reserves His most blistering condemnation for false spiritual leaders. As we study Matthew 23, we will see why they are such a great threat to Christianity.

The prophet Isaiah said, "The people will be like the priest" (Isa. 24:2, NASB*). He was saying that whatever a spiritual leader does, the people will do likewise. Jeremiah said, "The prophets prophesy falsely, and the priests bear rule by their means, and my people love to have it so" (Jer. 5:31). The Israelites loved what the false prophets told them. Later on in Jeremiah we read God's condemnation of those false spiritual leaders: "Many shepherds have destroyed my vineyard, they have trampled my portion under foot, they have made my pleasant portion a desolate wilderness" (Jer. 12:10). False spiritual leaders trample down the garden of God. People will follow those who lead them. False teachers have many people come to them for spiritual help, but they turn them away from the truth. That's why they are a severe threat.

New American Standard Bible.

B. The Denunciation from Christ

1. The subjects of the denunciation

In Matthew 23 the Lord Jesus confronts the false spiritual leaders of Israel—the scribes and the Pharisees—and reveals their true nature. First He warned the Jewish people not to be like them. He told the disciples to be true spiritual leaders by manifesting the attitudes of a true servant of God. Then from verse 13 on, the Lord turns from the crowd and the disciples to address the false spiritual leaders themselves. The crowd in the Temple court was large, as many people were visiting Jerusalem for the Passover season. The sermon recorded in Matthew 23 was Christ's last public sermon, and it dealt with an important subject. He warned the people to stay away from the false spiritual leaders because He knew they needed to avoid error if they were to follow the truth.

Christ's last public sermon wasn't a sermon on salvation or the power of God in a believer, nor was it a message on His resurrection. It was a message against false teachers. In the Sermon on the Mount, Christ's first recorded sermon, He said, "Beware of false prophets, who come to you in sheep's clothing, but inwardly they are ravening wolves" (Matt. 7:15). So Christ's first and last sermons as recorded by Matthew contained warnings about false spiritual leaders. That reminds us that society needs to be warned not only about Communism, humanism, secularism, and immorality but also about false spiritual leadership.

2. The specifics of the denunciation

The Lord bluntly stated that the Pharisees and scribes were false teachers because they lacked authority, integrity, sympathy, spirituality, and humility. As we will see in the next few lessons, Christ also stated why the Jewish religious leaders were in error, and He spoke of their impending judgment.

Christ's warning applies not only to His day but to our time as well. False spiritual leaders have always been around.

47

They are flourishing now in America because our society has been moving away from its Christian foundation. They've become more widespread in other parts of the world as well. Thus, people need to be warned about them. The apostle Paul warns the Ephesian elders about them in Acts 20: "Watch, and remember, that for the space of three years I ceased not to warn everyone night and day with tears" (v. 31). What did he warn them about? In verses 29-30 He says, "I know this, that after my departing shall grievous wolves enter in among you, not sparing the flock. Also of your own selves shall men arise, speaking perverse things."

So in Matthew 23 the Lord is calling people away from the scribes and Pharisees and is telling them to go to those who manifest the truth through their lives and message. He was trying to draw the people to His apostles. He knew He was going away, and He wanted to make sure people stayed away from the evil influence of the false spiritual leaders. Likewise, we must be warned today to follow true spiritual leaders, who seek not to be served but to serve. A true spiritual leader doesn't fleece the flock; he feeds it. He doesn't seek the highest honors. He recognizes that it's by the goodness of God that he has become great. Like Jesus, a true spiritual leader does not break a bruised reed or put out a smoldering wick (Matt. 12:20). We must follow true spiritual leaders who realize that the sheep are God's—and not their own to take advantage of.

Lesson

I. EXPLAINING THE CONDEMNATION

In verses 13-33 of Matthew 23, the Lord Jesus speaks directly to the Jewish religious leaders and pronounces seven curses on them. If you see eight curses in your Bible, that's because the curse in verse 14 is included in your version. The older manuscripts of the New Testament do not include verse 14, which means it was probably added later on. But that doesn't invalidate verse 14, because what it says is true. In fact, what probably happened is that a well-meaning scribe took Mark 12:40 or Luke 20:47 and inserted it in Matthew 23 because it fit the context so well. But based on the evidence of the older New Testament manuscripts, we won't include verse 14 in this study.

A. Its Two Main Characteristics

1. The expression of wrath

The seven curses pronounced by Christ made up a volatile scene. Imagine the shock everyone must have experienced when the Lord severely condemned the Jewish religious leaders in front of the Passover crowds. That kind of confrontation is foreign to us today. We resist condemning false spiritual leaders. Many Christians think it's unkind and ungracious to speak against any false religious system or spiritual leader. But that's a warped perspective; Jesus Himself strongly condemned false religious leaders. Some liberal theologians conveniently dismiss Jesus' criticism by saying that He wouldn't have said such things. But He did, and from His mouth came the most fearful, terrible words ever uttered on earth. The false leaders had rejected Christ and led the people astray. That was sufficient cause for divine judgment.

Matthew 23 is a serious chapter. Note the terms Jesus used to describe the false spiritual leaders. In several of the verses He calls them hypocrites. In verse 15 He says they are children of hell. In verse 17 He says they are foolish and blind. In verse 33 He says, "Ye serpents, ye generation of vipers, how can ye escape the damnation of hell?" Christ was using strong language. With a deadly calm and crushing power, He said things they did not want to hear.

2. The expression of sorrow

Yet in Christ's condemnation there is a sense of sorrow. He didn't give a scathing rebuke apart from any emotion. There is a certain melancholy that breaks forth in verse 37 as Jesus says, "O Jerusalem, Jerusalem, thou that killest the prophets, and stonest them who are sent unto thee, how often would I have gathered thy children together, even as a hen gathereth her chickens under her

49

wings, and ye would not!" On the day Jesus rode into Jerusalem upon a colt, He wept over the city (Luke 19:41). Christ felt pain when He declared judgment. In Matthew 23 we see the fiery, righteous indignation of God, yet we also see the Lord's sympathetic love as He speaks of the inevitable judgment.

B. Its Two Main Components

1. The word *woe*

One key word in Matthew 23:13-33 is the word *woe*. It appears seven times, each time in a distinctive context. "Woe" is a translation of the Greek word *ouai*, which sounds more like a painful cry than a word. It's an onomatopoetic word: it sounds like its meaning. The Greek word *ouai* is used in the Septuagint (the Greek translation of the Old Testament) to refer to grief, despair, sorrow, dissatisfaction, and pain. It's used in the New Testament to speak of sorrow and judgment and is translated "alas" in Revelation 18:16, where it speaks of the sad but inevitable judgment that will come upon the future Babylon. Condemnation and pity are mingled together in the word *woe*.

2. The word *hypocrite*

Another word that dominates the text in Matthew 23 is *hypocrite* (Gk., *hupokritēs*). It originally referred to an actor—someone who pretends to be something he isn't. The word didn't have any negative meaning at first, but in time it came to mean "deceiver." It refers to someone who looks good outwardly but is really evil. In Matthew 6 we read about the hypocrisy of the Jewish religious leaders. They gave money in an ostentatious way, prayed on the street corners, and fasted not for God's sake but to get attention from men. They appeared outwardly to be pious, but inwardly they weren't, so they were deceivers.

When Jesus used the word *woe* repetitively in Matthew 23, He wasn't wishing condemnation upon the Jewish religious leaders; He was speaking factually: divine judgment was inevitable. Jesus was informing them that they were already cursed.

False spiritual leaders face the same condemnation from God today as they did in Christ's time. Therefore, we need to deal with them in the same way. We need to be warned about false teachers just as the people in Matthew 23 were warned, and we need to warn others about them.

II. EXPRESSING THE CONDEMNATION

A. False Teachers Are Cursed for Their Exclusion (v. 13)

False spiritual leaders keep people out of God's kingdom. False religion doesn't help anyone. Don't say, "Non-Christian religious leaders are OK; they're doing what they think is best to try to help people with their problems. They set somewhat good moral standards for people to live by." False spiritual leaders keep people from getting into heaven.

1. The indictment of false spiritual leaders

Matthew 23:13 says, "Woe unto you, scribes and Pharisees, hypocrites! For ye shut up the kingdom of heaven against men; for ye neither go in yourselves, neither permit them that are entering to go in." That's the first statement Jesus made to the scribes and Pharisees, and it was a strong one.

Notice that the Lord said, "Ye shut up the kingdom of heaven against men." He said that out of irony because the Jewish leaders believed they were the ones who let people into the kingdom. They visualized themselves as having the keys to the kingdom because they thought they knew the way in. But in reality, they kept people out. The apostle Paul condemns the Jewish leaders when he says in Romans 2, "Thou art called a Jew, and resteth in the law, and makest thy boast of God, and knowest his will, and approvest the things that are more excellent, being instructed out of the law, and art confident that thou thyself art a guide of the blind, a light of them who are in darkness, an instructor of the foolish, a

51

teacher of babes, who hast the form of knowledge and of the truth in the law" (vv. 17-20). Then Paul said that they weren't what they thought they were because instead of glorifying God, they were actually blaspheming the name of God among the Gentiles (vv. 21-24). The Jewish leaders said they knew the truth and the law and that they were the light in the darkness. But they kept people out of heaven.

The phrase "the kingdom of heaven" in Matthew 23:13 means the sphere of salvation; it is the place where God rules. He rules over those who become saved and belong to Him—those who come to Him by grace through faith (Eph. 2:8-9). So to shut people out of the kingdom is to keep people from becoming saved.

2. The intervention by false spiritual leaders

Jesus said the Jewish leaders shut up the kingdom of heaven "against men." The phrase literally means "before men." He was saying that the religious leaders were slamming the doors of the kingdom right in people's faces. He was making a vivid statement. Christ wasn't talking about people who weren't interested in the kingdom; He was saying that the Jewish leaders were shutting the door on people who were trying to get in!

Jesus came into the world to tell people how to get into the kingdom. Prior to His teaching ministry, John the Baptist preached the kingdom message, telling people to repent of their sins because the kingdom of heaven was near. Matthew 3:5-6 says that people came to John the Baptist from the region all around the Jordan to be baptized and to confess their sins. They wanted to prepare their hearts for the Messiah; they were starting to make steps toward the kingdom by repenting of their sins and straightening out their lives.

When some Pharisees and Sadducees came to the Jordan while John the Baptist was baptizing, John said to them, "O generation of vipers, who hath warned you to flee from the wrath to come? Bring forth, therefore, fruits befitting repentance" (Matt. 3:7-8). John knew the religious leaders for what they really were; that's why he confronted them. There were many people around him getting ready to move toward the kingdom, and he didn't want the false teachers slamming the door of the kingdom in their faces.

a) The particulars

How specifically did the false religious leaders shut people off from the kingdom? By denying or misinterpreting the Word of God. They denied that Jesus was the Messiah and that salvation was by grace. Instead, they propagated a works-righteousness system that had no place for Christ, thereby keeping people out of the kingdom.

If I don't seem too excited about fighting humanism, secularism, immorality, or politics, it's because there's a much more important battle: that of clear and accurate articulation of the truth against the error of false spiritual leaders. We need to get Christians to know and declare what they believe and to confront error with boldness. The church needs to know the Word of God and to take its stand against false teachers.

b) The passages

(1) 1 Timothy 4:1

Paul told Timothy that false spiritual leaders teach the doctrines of demons.

(2) Luke 11:52

Jesus said, "Woe unto you, lawyers! For ye have taken away the key of knowledge; ye entered not in yourselves, and them that were entering in ye hindered." False religious leaders keep people from becoming saved, and we can't take that lightly. Don't be afraid to condemn them for fear of being unloving. Some liberal theologians say

Jesus was unkind to condemn the false teachers. But we have a mandate to act as He acted.

(3) Matthew 16:19

Jesus told Peter, "I will give unto thee the keys of the kingdom of heaven." Those who are true teachers—Peter, the apostles, and all those who follow in their doctrine—have the keys to the kingdom. They open the door to heaven and let people in, but false teachers shut the door in people's faces by their lies and false religion. I once asked one such teacher, "Doesn't it bother you that you never give people the saving gospel of Jesus Christ that can save them from eternal hell?" Men's souls are at stake in the hands of such people.

(4) John 9

In John 9 is the account of a man who was born blind so that God would be glorified when the man was healed. Jesus' healing him was a wonderful expression of divine power and compassion. When the Jewish religious leaders heard about the healing, they wanted an explanation of what had happened. They asked the man's parents, who responded, "He is of age; ask him. He shall speak for himself" (v. 21). They said that because they feared the Jewish leaders. Verse 22 says that the Jews "had agreed already that, if any man did confess that [Jesus] was Christ, he should be put out of the synagogue."

In verse 24 the Pharisees essentially tell the blind man, "You had better praise God for the healing, because Jesus is a sinner." When the healed man tried to explain who Jesus must be (vv. 30-33), the Pharisees rebuked him by saying, "Thou wast altogether born in sins, and dost thou teach us?" (v. 34). The end of verse 34 says they threw him out of the synagogue. They didn't want anyone who upset their theology.

(5) Acts 4:16-18

The Jewish religious leaders were damning the souls of people because they denied that Christ was the Messiah. In Acts 4 the Sanhedrin meets to discuss how they can keep Peter and John from preaching the gospel. They said, "What shall we do with these men? For that indeed a notable miracle hath been done by them is manifest to all those who dwell in Jerusalem; and we cannot deny it. But that it spread no further among the people, let us threaten them, that they speak henceforth to no man in this name. And they called them, and commanded them not to speak at all nor teach in the name of Jesus" (vv. 16-18). The Sanhedrin didn't want anything to do with Jesus.

(6) 1 Thessalonians 2:14-16

Paul wrote to the Thessalonians, warning about false religious leaders. Verse 14 talks about the persecution the Jewish Christians were receiving from the religious leaders, whom verse 15 says "killed the Lord Jesus and their own prophets." Paul said of them, "They please not God, and are contrary to all men, forbidding us to speak to the Gentiles, that they might be saved" (vv. 15-16).

A Necessary Confrontation

I'll never forget the day I received a phone call from a young man in my church who said he was going to become a Mormon. He told me some Mormons were coming to his house later on to talk to him about joining the church. I immediately got into my car and beat them to his house. I told him I wanted to confront them because they would lead him away from Christ. When the two Mormons arrived, I was in the spirit of Matthew 23—I pronounced curses upon them and told them everything God's Word says about those who deny Christ and His saving gospel. I wasn't in any mood to discuss doctrine or theology.

Every Christian should have the courage to speak the truth about false spiritual leaders if a situation calls for it. I doubt if the Mormon visitors will ever forget that encounter. But the Lord can use that to make them think about what they are doing. Sometimes we're lulled into thinking we shouldn't offend anyone, and we end up letting false teachers direct people toward eternal damnation.

Religious systems that teach salvation by works are the strongest opponents of the gospel of grace. Such systems are everywhere. It's a traumatic experience for me to see the religion section of the *Los Angeles Times* on Saturday because of all the spiritual phonies who advertise there. People who are seeking comfort and spiritual help from religious leaders often have the door to salvation slammed in their faces. That's tragic, and we can't afford to be tolerant of any religious system that leads to the condemnation of men's souls.

B. False Teachers Are Cursed for Their Perversion (v. 15)

1. The propagation of false religion

   False religious teachers not only keep people away from true religion but also end up corrupting them. Matthew 23:15 says, "Woe unto you, scribes and Pharisees, hypocrites! For ye compass sea and land to make one proselyte, and when he is made, ye make him twofold more the child of hell than yourselves." That's a strong statement.

   a) The scope of proselytization

   According to Jewish history, there was a great effort by the Jewish leaders to proselytize Gentiles during the life of our Lord. The word *proselyte* originally comes from a term that means "stranger." Here in Matthew 23:15 and in the book of Acts, the word is used to refer to converting someone. The Jewish religious leaders were aggressively proselytizing people during the New Testament era.

In the Old Testament, God chose Israel to be a channel to display Himself to the world. But the Israelites were reluctant to do so, which explains the peculiar response of the prophet Jonah. When the Gentile city of Nineveh repented and turned to God, Jonah wanted to die because he couldn't stand seeing Gentiles becoming saved (Jonah 4:1-3). The Jews had been provincial in their thinking, but that changed during Christ's time. In fact, we know historically that many synagogues at that time were attended by people who had left pagan religions to seek the true God. They were converts to Judaism. And in Matthew 23:15, Jesus speaks to the Pharisees and scribes about their traveling everywhere just to gain one convert.

b) The security in proselytizing

People within a false religious system are pleased when others join them because it gives them the feeling they must be right about their beliefs. Some cults flourish merely because each person involved feels secure from the number of other people involved. The Pharisees perhaps added people to their religion to cover their own doubt and turn it into some kind of confidence.

2. The participants in false religion

Commentator William Hendriksen said there were basically two kinds of proselytes: the proselyte of the gate and the proselyte of righteousness (*The Gospel of Matthew* [Grand Rapids: Baker, 1973], p. 829).

a) Those with cursory commitment

The proselyte of the gate was a Gentile who only attended the synagogue. He just barely got into the gate to the kingdom by stopping his worship of pagan deities and coming to the true God. In the book of Acts that type of person was known as a worshiper of God (16:14; 18:7), or someone who was devout (13:50; 17:4, 17).

b) Those with complete commitment

The proselyte of righteousness was the convert who became just as self-righteous and legalistic as the Jewish religious leaders. That was the kind of convert the Pharisees sought. But most of the converts to Judaism merely attended the synagogue, and very few became proselytes of righteousness. That's why the Lord says in Matthew 23:15, "Ye compass sea and land to make one proselyte." What's interesting is that a person who became an all-out convert was even given a Jewish name to cut him off from his past. He would also be circumcised and live in full adherence to Mosaic tradition.

3. The product of false religion

a) Described

What was the result of the proselytizing work of the Pharisees? Jesus said, "Ye make him twofold more the child of hell than yourselves" (v. 15). Have you ever noticed that a convert to a cult is often more zealous in his convictions than someone who was raised in it? In fact, that's even true in Christianity. Those who become saved from an ungodly background are usually zealous because of their newfound faith. There's something about a dramatic transition that creates a great amount of zeal.

The new converts were more fanatical than those who had been raised in the Judaistic religious system. They thought they had discovered the truth and had not been in the system long enough to learn the problems within it. Thus such converts became twice the sons of hell in the sense that they were even more zealous than their teachers in advocating false religion. Instead of finding God, the converts became people twice as hypocritical and damnable as the Pharisees and scribes. A child of hell is someone whose deeds characterize him as belonging to hell.

b) Depicted

The word *hell* in Matthew 23:15 is the translation of the Greek word *geenna*. Christ's use of the word had a special significance. There was a valley near Jerusalem known as the Valley of Hinnom. In the Old Testament era, those who worshiped the god Molech would burn their children alive as sacrifices in that valley (2 Chron. 28:3; Jer. 7:31). That valley, then, became identified with the worst kind of paganism. In 2 Kings 23:10, King Josiah declares the area unclean. It became a dump, and up through the time of Christ, trash burned there constantly. Thus the Valley of Hinnom became a symbol of eternal burning; it became synonymous with what hell is like and the burning of the waste of humanity. Christ said that when the religious leaders made a convert, he was twice the son of hell they were, speaking comparatively of the degree of hellish character as well as the degree of punishment.

False religious systems today are no different. They are a threat to the souls of men, and they must be confronted as such. Many people who are searching for God and the answers to life end up being herded into a false religion that shuts the door of God's kingdom in their faces. It is almost inconceivable to imagine the wrath God will pour out upon the false teachers who stand before Him at judgment someday.

A Christian's Call to Action

If you are a Christian, there are two things I'd like to bring to your mind.

1. Be thankful

You ought to be thankful that when you became a Christian, it was because the person who helped lead you to the Lord was a door opener and not a door closer. You're not in God's kingdom because of anything you did; you're in it because of God's grace. I thank God that I was raised in a Christian home with parents who taught me the truth. I also thank Him for letting me be exposed to the teaching of men of God and not to some false spiritual leader who would merely usher me to hell. We who are Christians should be grateful that we're in God's kingdom.

Sometimes Christians are too concerned about such things as not getting the seat they wanted at a banquet, not finding a parking space near the church, not liking the wallpaper in one of the rooms, or not liking the music or sermon. You need to keep a proper perspective: If you're going to a church that teaches the truth, then you should be grateful to God. You are responsible for praising and thanking God for wherever the truth is preached, lived, and believed—in spite of any imperfections.

2. Lead people to the kingdom

As a Christian, you have the keys to the kingdom, so you need to be calling people away from closed doors to the open one. You know how to enter the kingdom; now let others know.

If you are frank about false religious systems in your encounters with an unsaved person or with someone involved in false religion, you'll plant a thought that the person can't get away from. I've done that on several occasions to those who have come to my door to talk to me about their cult. I tell them that I'm not interested in hearing what they teach and let them know what Jesus said about those who teach false doctrines. I let them know that I'm happy to share the truth with them, but I don't want to hear their damning lies. That is much more powerful than letting such visitors think they have defeated you in a debate about biblical doctrine. You need to confront them. And when you do, ask the Spirit of God to guide you on how you should do that. We need to call people away from false religious systems—to pull them out of the fire (Jude 23).

Focusing on the Facts

1. What is the greatest threat facing the church today? Why (see p. 46)?
2. Describe the wrath Jesus expressed toward the scribes and Pharisees in Matthew 23. Why did He pronounce judgment on them (see p. 47)?
3. With what was Christ's condemnation mingled, as seen in Matthew 23:37 (see pp. 49-50)?
4. What is the word *woe* (Gk., *ouai*) used to refer to in the New Testament? What were some of the things the Pharisees did that made them hypocrites (see p. 50)?
5. What is significant about Christ's repeated use of the word *woe* in Matthew 23 (see pp. 50-51)?
6. Since false spiritual leaders face the same condemnation now as they did in Christ's time, how should we deal with them (see p. 51)?
7. How did the Jewish religious leaders visualize themselves in relation to their followers? What in fact were they really doing to their followers (Matt. 23:13; see pp. 51-52)?
8. What did John the Baptist say to the Pharisees and Sadducees who came to him? Why (Matt. 3:7-8; see pp. 52-53)?
9. How did the Jewish leaders shut people off from the kingdom (see p. 53)?
10. What do false spiritual leaders teach, according to 1 Timothy 4:1 (see p. 53)?
11. What did Paul say the Jewish religious teachers were doing in 1 Thessalonians 2:15-16 (see p. 55)?
12. To what extent did the Pharisees seek converts during Christ's time (see p. 56)?
13. Why do people within a cult like to have others join them (see p. 57)?
14. Describe two kinds of proselytes (see pp. 57-58).
15. What did Jesus say the Pharisees did to those whom they proselytized? Explain (Matt. 23:15; see p. 58).
16. Many people who are searching for _____ and the answers to _____ end up being herded into a false religion that shuts the door of _____ _____ in their faces (see p. 59).
17. As a Christian, what should you be thankful for? What should you be calling people to (see pp. 59-60)?

Pondering the Principles

1. What should you say when you are approached by people involved in a false religion? If they have no interest in letting you explain what you believe about Christ and the Bible, then it's better to refuse to get into a discussion. Should you happen to be in a situation where a discussion takes place, keep the length of the discussion minimal and stand strong against what they say without becoming argumentative. Some good things to do are to give your testimony, emphasizing that salvation is by grace and not works, and speak of the changes that have taken place in your life as a result of becoming a Christian. Another tremendous help is to be familiar with Scripture passages that affirm the authority of the Bible and the deity of Christ because those are the two issues almost all cults err on. Ask the Holy Spirit to make you sensitive about what you should say when you speak to people involved in a false religion. Above all, remember that your *best* defense is to know the Bible well. Although it may help to be familiar with the background of a cult, familiarity with the Bible itself will enable you to discern false teaching and correct it with the truth.

2. Something is happening today in Christianity that shouldn't be happening: many Christians shy away from testifying about Christ to others through their words or actions. Even worse, the members of many cults are overt in their attempt to gain converts. You may be the only Christian some of your acquaintances, family, or friends know. Remember, you are a Christian most likely because someone else spoke about Christ to you. Meditate on Matthew 5:13-16, and determine how Christ would want you to respond to His words in that passage. Memorize Matthew 5:16, and let it serve as a reminder to you to be a constant testimony for Christ: "Let your light so shine before men, that they may see your good works, and glorify your Father, who is in heaven."

4

The Condemnation of False Spiritual Leaders—Part 2

Outline

Introduction
A. The Reward for True Servants
B. The Rebuke for False Servants
Review
I. Explaining the Condemnation
II. Expressing the Condemnation
   A. False Teachers Are Cursed for Their Exclusion (v. 13)
   B. False Teachers Are Cursed for Their Perversion (v. 15)

Lesson
C. False Teachers Are Cursed for Their Subversion (vv. 16-22)
   1. The cover-up (v. 16)
      a) The reason for covering up
      b) The rebuke against covering up
         (1) In the Old Testament
         (2) In the New Testament
   2. The correction (vv. 17-19)
      a) Regarding the Temple (v. 17)
      b) Regarding the altar (vv. 18-19)
   3. The conclusion (vv. 20-22)
D. False Teachers Are Cursed for Their Inversion (vv. 23-24)
   1. They neglect to follow all God's commands
      a) The obsession
      b) The omission
      c) The obligation
   2. They neglect the sin in their lives

    E. False Teachers Are Cursed for Their Extortion (vv. 25-26)
       1. The reality behind false piety
       2. The requirement for true piety
    F. False Teachers Are Cursed for Their Deception (vv. 27-28)
       1. The action
       2. The analogy
    G. False Teachers Are Cursed for Their Pretension (vv. 29-32)
       1. The illusion (vv. 29-30)
       2. The indictment (vv. 31-32)
III. Exclaiming the Condemnation

Conclusion

Introduction

A. The Reward for True Servants

In the Bible, no one is so honored and respected as the true and faithful man of God. The testimonies of such servants appear throughout the pages of Scripture. The apostle Paul said that the Galatians received him "as an angel of God, even as Christ Jesus" (Gal. 4:14). When speaking of Epaphroditus, his beloved companion in service, Paul told the Philippians to "receive him . . . with all gladness, and hold such in reputation, because, for the work of Christ, he was near unto death" (Phil. 2:29-30). In 1 Thessalonians 5:12-13 Paul writes, "Know them who labor among you, and are over you in the Lord, and admonish you . . . esteem them very highly in love for their work's sake." First Timothy 5:17 says, "Let the elders that rule well be counted worthy of double honor," and Hebrews 13:17 says, "Obey them that have the rule over you, and submit yourselves; for they watch for your souls, as they that must give account, that they may do it with joy, and not with grief." Scripture extols the blessedness of those who are faithful; it speaks frequently of the reward of those who are true spiritual leaders.

B. The Rebuke for False Servants

In contrast, no one is so severely condemned as false spiritual leaders. The most furious words of judgment and wrath are reserved for those who parade themselves as representing God, when in fact they are liars and hypocrites. Scripture repeatedly warns about teachers who are void of the knowledge of God, who are strangers to the salvation they say they proclaim, who are starving while supposedly offering true bread, and who are warning men of a hell that they themselves will populate. Seventeenth-century preacher Richard Baxter wrote, "Many a tailor can go in rags while making costly clothes for others. Many a cook may scarcely lick his fingers when he has prepared the most sumptuous dishes for others to eat" (*The Reformed Pastor* [Portland, Oreg.: Multnomah, 1982], p. 28). False spiritual leaders appear to be clothing others with righteousness and feeding them the sustenance of God, but in reality they themselves have no clothes to offer and no food to give.

The scribes and Pharisees of the New Testament era were false spiritual leaders. In Matthew 23:13-36 Jesus rebukes them with unmitigated condemnation. Although the scribes and Pharisees are the only people Jesus condemns in Matthew 23, they stand as models of all other false spiritual leaders. We can learn much about false spiritual leaders by reading what Christ condemned them for and can apply the truths of Matthew 23 to the false religious leaders of our own time. It's not important in this lesson to name specific people or groups; rather, I want to give you the biblical criteria for evaluating religious leaders so that you can make those judgments on your own. You need to be discerning, so that you can give respect and honor to those who are true spiritual leaders and condemn those who are not.

Review

The account recorded in Matthew 23 took place on the Wednesday of Passion Week—two days before the crucifixion. When Jesus rode into Jerusalem on Monday and was hailed as the Messiah (Matt. 21:9), the Jewish religious leaders panicked. They despised Him because everything He taught was contrary to their doctrine. He lived a life they couldn't live and had a popularity they couldn't attain. His actions, knowledge, and words intimidated the religious leaders, and they wanted to eliminate Him. When the Lord came into the city on Tuesday and cleansed the Temple (Matt. 21:12-13), their anger turned into rage. In Matthew 21:28—22:14 Jesus pronounces judgment on them through three parables, saying that the Jewish leaders would be shut out of the kingdom. Then He answered three questions from His enemies and made them look foolish. By that time they were in a frenzy, and we can better understand why they had Him crucified two days later.

Wednesday's dialogue with the Jewish religious leaders ended with the sermon in Matthew 23. In fact, it was the last public sermon our Lord preached. In it, He warned the people to stay away from false spiritual leaders (vv. 1-12), condemned the religious leaders (vv. 13-36), and lamented over the consequence of Israel's unbelief (vv. 37-39)—the latter being the unfortunate legacy of false spiritual leaders. In His blistering sermon, Christ told the people that the scribes and Pharisees lacked authority, integrity, sympathy, spirituality, and humility. Then He turned to the religious leaders themselves and confronted them.

I. EXPLAINING THE CONDEMNATION (see pp. 48-51)

Seven times in Matthew 23 Jesus uses the word translated "woe" (Gk., *ouai*), which is not really translatable. It's more of an onomatopoetic sound uttered from deep within in a moment of pain or grief. The curses Christ pronounced were not merely what He wished would happen; they were divine decrees. He was pronouncing final judgment on the religious leaders of Israel for rejecting Him and leading the nation of Israel to reject Him. There are seven curses pronounced by Christ in verses 13-36.

II. EXPRESSING THE CONDEMNATION

A. False Teachers Are Cursed for Their Exclusion (v. 13; see pp. 51-56)

Jesus says in Matthew 23:13, "Woe unto you, scribes and Pharisees, hypocrites! For ye shut up the kingdom of heaven against men; for ye neither go in yourselves, neither permit them that are entering to go in." The phrase "them that are entering" refers to people who were endeavoring to enter the kingdom. In Matthew 3 John the Baptist is preparing such people for the arrival of the Messiah. People were coming from Jerusalem and Judea to confess their sins and repent of them. They were being baptized, showing outwardly their inward desire to be pure and ready when the Messiah arrived. But the scribes and Pharisees shut the door to the kingdom in those people's faces.

False spiritual leaders are not to be thought of as well-intentioned but misguided people who are leading mankind to moral behavior. They are shutting the door to salvation in people's faces. They teach heresy and must be treated in a manner consistent with the damage they do.

B. False Teachers Are Cursed for Their Perversion (v. 15; see pp. 56-60)

False spiritual leaders pervert those who come under their influence. They not only shut people out of heaven but also usher them into hell. People come to them seeking moral change, emotional or psychological help, and spiritual guidance only to become children of hell.

Matthew 23:15 says, "Woe unto you, scribes and Pharisees, hypocrites! For ye compass sea and land to make one proselyte, and when he is made, ye make him twofold more the child of hell than yourselves." A proselyte was originally someone who came into Palestine to live with the Jews, but by Christ's time, it referred to a Gentile who embraced the Jewish religion. The proselytes Jesus was speaking about weren't those who just took on a few of the elements of Judaism but those who became full-fledged, legalistic, ritualistic, hair-splitting Pharisees filled with fanatical zeal. Jesus was saying that the Pharisees sought to make their converts just like themselves, and as a result, they made them into double the sons of hell.

67

C. False Teachers Are Cursed for Their Subversion (vv. 16-22)

The Jewish religious leaders developed a style of reasoning that undermined the truth. Anyone who is of God is characterized by truth because God is a God of truth. Paul says in Titus 1:2 that God cannot lie. In fact, He hates lying and anything that is false. In John 8:44, our Lord says the devil is a liar and the father of lies. False religious systems are filled with lies and broken promises.

Leaders with No Sense of Direction

Instead of calling the Pharisees hypocrites in verse 16, Jesus calls them blind guides, because they lived under the illusion that they were guides for the spiritually blind. Romans 2 says the Jewish religious leaders were confident that they were "a guide of the blind, a light of them who are in darkness, an instructor of the foolish, a teacher of babes, who hast the form of knowledge and of the truth in the law" (vv. 19-20). Jesus was telling the religious leaders in Matthew 23:16 that they thought they were giving wisdom to the foolish, but they themselves didn't even know the truth. In Matthew 15:14 He tells them this: "[You] are blind leaders of the blind. And if the blind lead the blind, both shall fall into the ditch." Christ's accusation was shocking because the Jewish leaders were proud of their supposed spiritual sight and ability to guide people.

1. The cover-up (v. 16)

Jesus says in Matthew 23:16, "Woe unto you, ye blind guides, who say, Whosoever shall swear by the temple, it is nothing; but whosoever shall swear by the gold of the temple, he is a debtor!"

a) The reason for covering up

To understand that statement, we need to keep in mind that all false spiritual leaders are liars. Only those who possess the life of God can be true; only God can break down a fallen man's tendency to lie. That's a part of God's redemptive work.

To cover their lies and appear pious, the scribes and Pharisees developed a system by which they could lie with impunity. They would make promises or vows and confirm that they would keep their promises by making a contract of some kind—but they included a way of getting out of the promise if they needed to. Every culture has its own way of making people keep their promises. Some people seal a promise in blood, or in a written contract. In the New Testament era, people would swear by their promises. In a society where lying was prolific, the recipient of a promise had to protect himself and have some way of making the promisor keep his word.

b) The rebuke against covering up

Jesus addressed the problem of people's not keeping their promises in Matthew 5. He said, "Swear not at all. . . . But let your communication be, Yea, yea; nay, nay; for whatever is more than these cometh of evil" (vv. 34, 37). When a person of integrity says yes, that's exactly what he means, or when he says no, that's exactly what he means. A truthful person doesn't need to "swear on a stack of Bibles" or say, "Cross my heart and hope to die." Some people say that if they cross their fingers when making a vow, they don't have to keep the vow.

The system of swearing that the scribes and Pharisees adhered to allowed them to lie, and their promises came to mean nothing. They could make a vow in front of many people that they would give God a certain amount of money, then later on say, "I only swore by such-and-such; therefore, I don't have to give God the full amount I promised." In Matthew 23:16 Christ denounces the scribes and Pharisees because they were saying, "If you swear by the Temple, that's nothing, but if you swear by the gold of the Temple, then you have to keep your promise." Apparently the Jewish religious leaders attached significance to the gold when making vows. But it was simply a convenient way to get out of keeping a promise.

(1) In the Old Testament

The Old Testament says we are to keep our promises. God hates lying.

(a) Psalm 50:14—"Offer unto God thanksgiving, and pay thy vows unto the Most High." Don't make promises to God that you can't keep.

(b) Psalm 56:12—"Thy vows are upon me, O God; I will render praises unto thee." David said he was bound by his promises to the Lord.

(c) Psalm 61:8—"So will I sing praise unto thy name forever, that I may daily perform my vows."

(d) Psalm 66:13—"I will go into thy house with burnt offerings; I will pay thee my vows."

(e) Psalm 76:11—"Vow, and pay unto the Lord your God."

(2) In the New Testament

In Acts 5 a couple named Ananias and Sapphira vow to give the Lord all the proceeds from the sale of a piece of property. But when they saw how much money they got from the property, they changed their minds and decided to keep part of the money (vv. 1-2). Do you know what happened as a result of their breaking the vow they made to God? The Lord killed both of them in front of the whole congregation of the early church in Jerusalem (vv. 5, 10-11).

2. The correction (vv. 17-19)

   a) Regarding the Temple (v. 17)

   In Matthew 23:17 Jesus doesn't even address the immorality of the scribes and Pharisees' word games;
   instead He exposes the illogical reasoning behind
   them. He said, "Ye fools and blind; for which is
   greater, the gold, or the temple that sanctifieth the
   gold?" The only reason the gold of the Temple could
   be thought of as sacred was that it was of the Temple—the dwelling place of God. The Jewish religious
   leaders were using ridiculous logic as grounds for violating their promises.

   b) Regarding the altar (vv. 18-19)

   In verses 18-19 our Lord gives another example of
   their deceptive reasoning: "And [you say], Whosoever shall swear by the altar, it is nothing; but whosoever sweareth by the gift that is upon it, he is bound.
   Ye fools and blind; for which is greater, the gift, or
   the altar that sanctifieth the gift?" He was saying,
   "Your logic is ridiculous; it doesn't make sense. It's
   only when the gift is offered to God on the altar that
   it means something." The scribes and Pharisees
   thought that when they made vows with objects that,
   in their minds, were not overtly connected with God,
   they could break their vows. Yet false spiritual
   leaders often devise such systems for themselves because they lie all the time. They need a way to protect
   themselves whenever they want to break a promise.

3. The conclusion (vv. 20-22)

   Jesus says in Matthew 23:20-22, "Whosoever, therefore,
   shall swear by the altar, sweareth by it, and by all things
   on it. And whosoever shall swear by the temple, sweareth by it, and by him that dwelleth in it. And he that
   shall swear by heaven, sweareth by the throne of God,
   and by him who sitteth on it." Ultimately, no matter
   what a person swears by, it will connect in some way to
   God. It didn't matter what the scribes and Pharisees
   swore by—a gift on the altar itself, the gold of the Tem-

ple, the Temple itself, the heavens, or the throne of God, for God is the Creator of all and Lord over all. Thus, the religious leaders were supposed to be truthful.

False spiritual leaders don't tell the truth. Instead, they act pious so as to cover up their lying. Peter said, "Through covetousness shall they, with feigned words, make merchandise of you" (2 Pet. 2:3). They say they need money when they don't need it. They say God told them something when God never told them anything. They say Jesus led them to do something when in reality He did not. Beware of the lies of false spiritual leaders.

D. False Teachers Are Cursed for Their Inversion (vv. 23-24)

False spiritual leaders are guilty of reversing divine priorities.

1. They neglect to follow all God's commands

   a) The obsession

      Jesus says in Matthew 23:23, "Woe unto you, scribes and Pharisees, hypocrites! For ye pay tithe [i.e., 10 percent] of mint and anise and cummin."

      Mint is a small leafy plant. The anise referred to here is dill, and was used in making dill pickles. Cumin is a tiny seed. All three items were used for flavoring food.

      In the Old Testament law, God instructed His people to give one-tenth of all their crops or produce every year to the treasury in Israel (Lev. 27:30). Because it went toward supporting the government, it was a form of taxation. There was also a second tenth to be paid every year for ceremonies and national festivals (Deut. 12:10-11, 17-18), and a third tenth every three years for strangers and poor people (Deut. 14:28-29). That means the Israelites were taxed about 23 percent of what they earned.

      In Deuteronomy 14:22, we read that the Israelites were to tithe "all the increase of thy seed." When God said that, He was referring to things like wheat, vegetables, wine, and olive oil. But the scribes and Pharisees, being the literalists that they were, went to the extreme to carefully count things like mint, dill, and cumin seeds. They made sure God got one seed for every nine that they kept. The Jewish religious leaders applied God's command to the most minuscule of things. Why did they do it? It made them feel pious.

b) The omission

Jesus told the scribes and Pharisees that while they were faithful to carefully count herb seeds, they had omitted the weightier matters of the law, such as justice, mercy, and faith (Matt. 23:23). False religious leaders get wrapped up in inconsequential details and have no capacity to deal with the essential matters of God's law. Jesus borrowed the word translated "weightier" in verse 23 from rabbinical terminology. The Jewish rabbis believed there were light elements of the law and heavy elements. Christ told them they were overlooking the weighty elements of justice, mercy, and faith.

Our Lord didn't just mention justice, mercy, and faith at random. Micah 6:8 says, "What doth the Lord require of thee, but to do justly, and to love mercy, and to walk humbly [faithfully] with thy God?" The Lord wanted the religious leaders to be just, merciful, and faithful, but they were unjust, unmerciful, unforgiving, and unkind. They abused the people by piling heavy burdens on them and not moving a finger to help lighten the load (Matt. 23:4). They were great at counting out seeds used to flavor food, but they overlooked what was really important: justice, mercy, and faith. False religious leaders get wrapped up in the minute details of their religious systems and forget about the things that really matter.

c) The obligation

Jesus says at the end of Matthew 23:23, "These ought ye to have done, and not to leave the other undone."

He was saying that the scribes and Pharisees should have been just, merciful, and faithful in addition to keeping the other parts of the law, such as tithing. And I don't think He was referring specifically to counting seeds but simply to the fact that they should tithe their crops and produce in general, as stated in the Old Testament. He didn't want them to concentrate on justice, mercy, and faith at the expense of tithing seeds. There was a proper place for tithing because the Jews were still under the obligation to obey the commandments relative to their national identity and form of government. God's ceremonial law wasn't set aside until the church was born.

Are We Still Obliged to Tithe Today?

Tithing is mentioned six times in the New Testament. The three times it is mentioned in the gospels, it always appears in a text condemning the scribes and Pharisees regarding their abuse of tithing. It is mentioned three more times in the book of Hebrews in reference to its role in Israel's history prior to the New Testament era. There is no place in the New Testament where tithing is ever commanded as a pattern of giving in the church. It was solely a form of taxation used to support the government of Israel.

I'm always amazed at how false religious systems have so much minutiae and so little reality. I think about that whenever I read of a "holy war" going on in the name of religion. We see such warring going on today in the Middle East between the different Islamic sects, as well as in Ireland between so-called Christians. The life-styles of such people betray that they have no commitment to the things that really matter. They actually massacre others in the name of their religions.

I know of a religious leader who has made many charts explaining all the details of Bible prophecy. He has explanations about all the details in the book of Revelation, but he's living in a state of adultery. He should burn his charts and stop living in sin. His perspective isn't right; like all false spiritual leaders, he is dealing with the minutiae and not the more important spiritual matters.

2. They neglect the sin in their lives

Christ gave another illustration of how the scribes and Pharisees had inverted their spiritual priorities. In Matthew 23:24 He says they were blind guides who "strain out a gnat and swallow a camel" (NASB). The the word *strain* (Gk., *diulizō*) means "to filter," and the smallest unclean creature that fit the description of unclean creatures in the Old Testament was a gnat (Lev. 11:41-43). The largest unclean creature the Jewish people were forbidden to eat was a camel (Lev. 11:4).

When wine was made in biblical times, occasionally a gnat would fly into the winepress as the grapes were being crushed. Or sometimes a gnat would fly into a cup of wine and get trapped in the liquid. The fastidious Pharisees didn't want to accidentally swallow a gnat, so they drank their wine with their teeth clenched shut. Should their be any gnats, they would be able to pick them off their teeth. So instead of enjoying what they were drinking, they were busy avoiding defilement by straining out gnats. So when Jesus told them they strained out gnats and swallowed camels, He was saying that their spiritual priorities were inverted. They were concerned about trivial matters and blind to the more important things. They allowed hypocrisy, dishonesty, cruelty, and greed to go unchecked in their lives.

Religious people can be so fastidious, yet be so far from what God seeks of them. False spiritual leaders reverse divine priorities by substituting the essential realities of the heart with insignificant, external rituals.

E. False Teachers Are Cursed for Their Extortion (vv. 25-26)

Verse 25 says, "Woe unto you, scribes and Pharisees, hypocrites! For ye make clean the outside of the cup and of the platter [a plate used to serve delicacies], but within they are full of extortion and excess."

1. The reality behind false piety

   The scribes and Pharisees were going around supposedly offering people lovely meals. They would serve a plate full of delicacies and a cup with the fruit of the vine. The plate and the cup had been ceremonially cleansed, but the food on the plate and the wine in the cup were stolen produce. The religious leaders would piously say, "We've ceremonially prepared the platter and the cup," but the food and wine they used was gained by extortion.

   There are many false spiritual leaders today who appear to offer sustenance of some kind to their followers, yet the sustenance they offer was really stolen from the people to whom they offer it. They milk their followers for everything they can get out of them.

   The Greek word translated "extortion" in verse 25 is the word *harpagē*, which means "to plunder" or "to rape." False spiritual leaders plunder people—making merchandise out of them for their own gain. The word translated "excess" (Gk., *akrasia*) means "an unrestrained desire for gain." The scribes and Pharisees lacked self-control. They were greedy robbers who plundered the souls, minds, and money of everyone in their grasp.

2. The requirement for true piety

   Jesus says in verse 26, "Thou blind Pharisee, cleanse first that which is within the cup and platter, that the outside of them may be clean also." He was saying, "You had better make sure that what's on your plate is as clean as the plate itself. A dish that holds food gained dishonestly is not clean." False spiritual leaders today parade their supposed piety, but they become rich and fat because they are thieves at heart.

F. False Teachers Are Cursed for Their Deception (vv. 27-28)

   Verse 27 says, "Woe unto you, scribes and Pharisees, hypocrites! For ye are like whited sepulchers, which indeed appear beautiful outward, but are within full of dead men's bones, and of all uncleanness." He was saying that they were guilty of deception and that they contaminated everyone they touched.

1. The action

On the fifteenth of Adar (during the month of March), the Jewish religious leaders of the New Testament era carried out an unusual ritual. By that time of year, the spring rains had ended. The rain washed away many things, including any whitewash that had been used on walls and houses. The ritual was this: the leaders would whitewash the limestone caves and tombs where people were buried. They did that to keep a traveler on his way to Jerusalem for the Passover from inadvertently touching a tomb and becoming defiled. When a person became defiled, he had to go through a ceremonial cleansing. To have to go through that immediately prior to the Passover season would mean exclusion from participating in certain Passover activities. In some cases the whole tomb was whitewashed; in others, they painted white bones on the tomb to identify what it was. Thus visitors coming into Jerusalem would see clean, white tombs everywhere, dazzling in the sun.

2. The analogy

Even though the tombs were whitewashed and looked beautiful, that didn't change what they were. Anyone who touched them was contaminated, regardless of the whitewash. Jesus says in Matthew 23:27 that the Jewish leaders were whited tombs that "indeed appear beautiful outward, but are within full of dead men's bones, and of all uncleanness." Then in verse 28, Jesus adds, "Even so ye also outwardly appear righteous unto men, but within ye are full of hypocrisy and iniquity." The scribes and Pharisees were filled with disregard for the law of God. They looked pure externally, but they contaminated everyone who touched them.

G. False Teachers Are Cursed for Their Pretension (vv. 29-32)

1. The illusion (vv. 29-30)

False spiritual leaders are cursed for pretending to be better than everyone else. Our Lord says in verse 29,

77

"Woe unto you, scribes and Pharisees, hypocrites! Because ye build the tombs of the prophets, and garnish the sepulchers of the righteous." The scribes and Pharisees were always lifting up the heroes of the past and memorializing them. Then Jesus said, "[You] say, If we had been in the days of our fathers, we would not have been partakers with them in the blood of the prophets" (v. 30). They were saying that they would have never killed the prophets as their fathers did. They thought they were much more holy.

The spiritual pride of the Jewish leaders was ugly. They were great at building monuments, honoring men of the past, and claiming to be better than others. In Matthew 21 Jesus says that the people of Israel had killed all the prophets of God in the parable of the vineyard and the landowner (vv. 33-44). But the religious leaders were claiming they would never do that.

2. The indictment (vv. 31-32)

Jesus' response to the religious leaders' claim in verse 31 was direct: "Wherefore, ye are witnesses against yourselves, that ye are the sons of them who killed the prophets." Jesus pointed out that they themselves admitted they were the sons of those who killed the prophets. Why did He say that? Because they had been, in fact, plotting to kill Jesus. They were so consumed with their own lying deceit that they didn't even realize they were plotting the death of the One greater than the prophets: the Son of God.

Verse 32 continues, "Fill up, then, the measure of your fathers." He was saying, "Go ahead and kill Me. You're scheming to kill the greatest prophet of all. That would be the fullest expression of the murderous attitude of the Israelites toward God's messengers." Jesus clearly states in that verse that they were going to take His life. They weren't any better than their fathers; in fact, they were worse.

III. EXCLAIMING THE CONDEMNATION

In verse 33 Jesus pronounces a curse on the scribes and Pharisees: "Ye serpents, ye generation of vipers, how can ye escape the damnation of hell?" He wasn't asking a question; He was saying there was no way they would escape the punishment of hell.

Conclusion

False spiritual leaders keep people out of heaven, but a true spiritual leader brings people into heaven. False teachers lead people to hell and make them double the sons of hell, but true spiritual leaders make men righteous. False spiritual leaders subvert the truth, but a true spiritual leader leads people into the truth. False spiritual leaders appear to be pious, but they use people for their own gain, whereas a true spiritual leader serves people and meets their needs. False teachers contaminate everyone they touch, but a true teacher makes holy anyone he touches. And finally, false religious leaders say they are better than everyone else, but true spiritual leaders say, as Paul did, that they are the least of all (Eph. 3:8) and know it's only by the grace of God that they are what they are (1 Cor. 15:10). God help us to be true spiritual leaders and avoid false spiritual leaders.

Focusing on the Facts

1. What kind of man is highly honored in Scripture? Who are the most severely condemned people in God's Word (see pp. 64-65)?
2. Although the scribes and Pharisees are the only people Jesus condemns in Matthew 23, they stand as _____ of all other false spiritual leaders (see p. 65).
3. What kind of reasoning had the Jewish religious leaders developed to justify their lies (Matt. 23:16; see p. 68)?
4. What does Scripture say about God in regard to lying (see p. 68)?
5. Why was Jesus' accusation that the Pharisees were blind guides leading the blind so shocking (see p. 68)?

6. What is Jesus basically saying in His statement in Matthew 5:34, 37 (see p. 69)?
7. What do various verses from Scripture teach about vows (see p. 70)?
8. How were the Pharisees and scribes violating their promises (Matt. 23:17-19; see p. 71)?
9. What does Jesus say about the way the Pharisees and scribes bound themselves to a vow in Matthew 23:20-22 (see pp. 71-72)?
10. Explain how the Jewish religious leaders had inverted their priorities (Matt. 23:23; see pp. 72-73).
11. What did Christ mean when He said the Jewish leaders "strain out a gnat and swallow a camel" (Matt. 23:24, NASB; see p. 75)?
12. Where does much of the sustenance that false spiritual leaders appear to offer their followers come from (see p. 76)?
13. Describe the yearly Jewish tradition Jesus is referring to in Matthew 23:27, and explain the analogy He makes in verses 27-28 (see pp. 76-77).
14. What did the scribes and Pharisees say about themselves in relation to God's prophets (Matt. 23:30)? How does Jesus respond to their claim in verses 31-32 (see p. 78)?
15. Describe what a true spiritual leader does, based on Christ's statements about false spiritual leaders in Matthew 23:13-32 (see p. 79).

Pondering the Principles

1. True spiritual leaders are honored by God, and we are to be grateful for them. Read Hebrews 13:17. Church leaders are accountable to God for how they lead the flock. It's a sobering responsibility, and a painful one, when a pastor or leader invests his life in people who do not grow or walk in the truth. Hebrews 13:17 says church leaders should be able to do their work with joy. It's sad when people in a church rob their pastor of the joy that comes with being a faithful minister. Think of several things a churchgoer could do to help his pastor minister with joy. What one specific action can you take this week that will encourage your pastor?

2. Read the comparison between false and true spiritual leaders
   on page 79. Which of the characteristics of a true spiritual
   leader have you seen in action in the leaders of your church?
   What specifically did the leader do? Take time now to write a
   note of thanks to one or more of the leaders in your church,
   and specify what things in his life you're thankful for. Also,
   make a habit of praying regularly for those who lead your
   church.

5

Jesus' Last Words to Israel— Part 1

Outline

Introduction
A. The Anticipation for the Messiah
B. The Antagonism Toward the Messiah
C. The Announcement from the Messiah
  1. To the people
  2. To the religious leaders
    a) The fiery curses
    b) The final condemnation
      (1) The cup of God's wrath
      (2) The cause of God's wrath
      (3) The characterization of God's wrath
    c) The frightful conclusion

Lesson
 I. The Imminent Condemnation (vv. 34-36)
    A. The Consequence of Israel's Rejection
      1. The identity of those being sent
      2. The intent for their being sent
    B. The Confirmation of Israel's Rejection
      1. The prophecy
      2. The purpose
    C. The Comprehensiveness of Israel's Rejection

1. The principle of cumulative guilt
    a) The accountability of the religious leaders
        (1) The explanation about their accountability
        (2) The extent of their accountability
    b) The animosity of the religious leaders
    c) The accusation against the religious leaders
2. The promise to the current generation

Introduction

In Matthew 23 appears one of the saddest scenes in the Bible: Christ's pronouncement of doom on the nation of Israel. The Israelites were condemned because as a whole they rejected Jesus Christ. In rejecting Him, they rejected God and His Word. The people who led the nation to reject Christ were false spiritual leaders known as the scribes and the Pharisees.

A. The Anticipation for the Messiah

For centuries the Jews waited for the arrival of their Messiah. They looked forward to the day when He would come to establish His kingdom—a kingdom where they would know blessedness. Many Jewish mothers hoped they would be the mother of the Messiah, and many Jewish men hoped to have a prominent position of honor and service within Messiah's kingdom. Yet when the Messiah came, instead of believing in Him they rejected Him and ultimately had Him executed. They also sought to kill all those who represented Him. It's an ironic twist to the history of Israel that the people were chosen by God's grace and given promises and hope, yet when the fulfillment of their greatest hope was to come to fruition in the arrival of the Messiah, they rejected and executed Him.

B. The Antagonism Toward the Messiah

Matthew 23 marks the climax of Christ's ministry to Israel. He preached the gospel to the Jewish people and gave them an opportunity to repent of their sins and believe in Him. They didn't do so as a whole, so in Matthew 23 Jesus confirms that their rejection is final. That rejection was initiated by the scribes and Pharisees. They were false spiritual leaders who had captured the hearts and minds of the people and turned them away from Jesus Christ. It is they whom Jesus condemns in this final public statement. He pronounced a message of damnation against the false teachers for leading the Jewish people astray.

C. The Announcement from the Messiah

1. To the people

In the first twelve verses of Matthew 23, Jesus warns the people to stay away from the false spiritual leaders. There was still hope for some people. Jesus knew that after He was crucified and resurrected there would be preachers of the gospel going through the land of Israel. There was still hope that some individuals would listen to the preachers and not the scribes and Pharisees. Although the sermon in Matthew 23 is a message of damnation on the nation as a whole, there were still some individuals who could be reached for Christ.

2. To the religious leaders

In Matthew 23:13-33 Jesus confronts the religious leaders with seven curses—right in front of the crowd. That was a bold action; He held back nothing.

a) The fiery curses

The Lord cursed the false spiritual leaders for exclusion—for keeping people out of heaven (v. 13). In verse 15 He curses them for perversion. They were making their converts twice the sons of hell that they themselves were. He cursed them for subverting the truth and substituting it with a system of lies (vv. 16-22). He also cursed them for inverting spiritual priorities. They placed unimportant rituals high on their list of priorities but overlooked weightier matters such as justice, mercy, and faith (vv. 23-24). In verses 25-26 He curses them for extortion. They looked pious externally, but in reality they were robbing their followers every chance they had. He then cursed them for deception because they appeared to be models of virtue when they were really contaminating people with their defilement (vv. 27-28). Finally, the Lord cursed them for pretension. They pretended to be holier than all those who preceded them, when in fact they were worse (vv. 29-31).

b) The final condemnation

(1) The cup of God's wrath

The climax of the Lord's condemnation of the false spiritual leaders appears in verse 32: "Fill up, then, the measure of your fathers." In Scripture, the phrase "fill up" is frequently used in connection with sin, judgment, and wrath. The image of a cup being filled to the brim is used in connection with God's divine wrath in Isaiah 51:17, Jeremiah 25:15, Habakkuk 2:16, and Revelation 16:19. Jesus referred to the cup of God's wrath when He said to the Father, "If it be possible, let this cup pass from me" (Matt. 26:39). Sin brings the wrath of God, which brings His divine judgment. God allows people to sin only so much, and then the cup of wrath is filled up and judgment is declared.

So in Matthew 23:32 Jesus was saying to the false religious leaders, "Do the rest of the evil that has to be done so that the cup of wrath will be filled and poured out in judgment against you." It's amazing to think that the Lord Jesus Christ, as holy as He is, would command anyone to do evil. But He did in that situation. He does the same thing in John 13:27 when He tells Judas, "What thou doest, do quickly." Jesus doesn't want evil to be done, but in those two situations He knew evil would be done, so He wanted it to be over with. He wanted the scribes and Pharisees to finish filling up the cup of Israel's sin so that judgment might come.

Notice what He called the cup: "the measure of your fathers." He was telling them to fill up the cup their fathers had been filling. Throughout Israel's history, there were people in the nation who were filling up the cup of inevitable judgment. Successive generations in the past had been filling the cup; thus the wickedness of each generation contributed to the final result. The Lord was saying in Matthew 23 that the brim of the cup had almost been reached. God's tolerance has its limits. In Genesis 6:3 God says, "My Spirit shall not always strive with man." Immediately afterward He covered the whole world with a flood, leaving only the eight people in Noah's family.

In the book of Revelation, the terrors of the Tribulation and the coming of the Lord Jesus Christ in final judgment are the result of man's sinfulness filling up the cup of wrath. There comes a point when God will not tolerate any more sin. There is only so much wickedness before judgment comes, and that's what was happening with the nation of Israel in Matthew 23. That's why Jesus told the scribes and Pharisees to finish off the cup—so that judgment would come soon.

(2) The cause of God's wrath

The scribes and Pharisees committed the same murderous sins their fathers did. In Matthew 23:30 they say, "If we had been in the days of our fathers, we would not have been partakers with them in the blood of the prophets." They were saying they wouldn't have slaughtered righteous men of God as their ancestors did. But Jesus said, "Ye are witnesses against yourselves, that ye are the sons of them who killed the prophets" (v. 31). The Lord knew the scribes and Pharisees were plotting His death. He was saying, "Who are you kidding? You are the sons of those who killed God's prophets, and you are ready to kill Me, the supreme prophet and the Messiah." The Jewish religious leaders claimed to be better than others, but they weren't. They were filling the same cup their fathers filled. What a terrible climax to the history of Israel.

Israel doesn't stand alone in her guilt; people have always killed righteous men. That's because righteous men live as a rebuke to society. If a society is lax enough to permit the killing of a righteous man, it will continue to do so—unless that society turns to God.

(3) The characterization of God's wrath

In Matthew 23:33, Jesus characterizes the false religious leaders by saying to them, "Ye serpents, ye generation of vipers [Gk., *echidna*]." *Echidna* refers to a small, poisonous snake. Jesus was characterizing them as a brood of poisonous snakes. The snake He referred to looked like a small twig or stick and lived in Israel's deserts. Sometimes a person who was gathering sticks for a fire would reach for one of those snakes, thinking it was a twig, and get bitten. That happened to Paul (Acts 28:3-5), and God miraculously spared him from the effects of the bite. Those vipers were almost impossible to distinguish, and they were deadly.

Interestingly, John the Baptist says the same thing about the religious leaders in Matthew 3:7. And they hadn't changed in the time between Matthew 3 to Matthew 23. John the Baptist's ministry had no effect on them, nor did Christ's ministry. They were hardened all the more as time went along; they were the same poisonous, deceitful snakes they were when Jesus first arrived. The Greek word *echidna* was connected with wickedness. In classic Greek mythology there was a monster by that name who was half snake and half woman. She gave birth to many other monsters. So the *echidna* was known as a wicked, deadly, deceitful creature. It was no compliment to be called an *echidna*.

c) The frightful conclusion

In verse 33 Jesus says, "Ye serpents, ye generation of vipers, how can ye escape the damnation of hell

[Gk., *geenna*]?" The word *geenna* came from Jerusalem's Valley of Gehenna, which is where the trash of the city was constantly being burned. The valley became a symbol for eternal hell. There was no way the religious leaders could avoid their fate.

Christ's description of the scribes and Pharisees as vipers trying to escape the flames of hell was an illustration the people of that time were familiar with. Whenever a farmer burned the stubble on his land or there was a brush fire, the snakes would come out of their holes and try to outrace the fire. They were never fast enough to escape, and that's how it will be for the scribes and Pharisees. As John the Baptist says in Matthew 3:7, they won't be able to flee from the wrath of God to come.

It's tragic that the people whom God called to minister His holy Word had become perverted as time went along. Even though they were holding God's true law in their hands, they were nothing more than snakes who deceived and poisoned a nation of people. Jesus said they would never escape the damnation of hell. And He wasn't talking to the criminals of Jewish society; He was talking to the *religious* leaders.

Lesson

I. THE IMMINENT CONDEMNATION (vv. 34-36)

A. The Consequence of Israel's Rejection

Verse 34 begins with the word *wherefore*. That word indicates Jesus is referring back to what He had said about the scribes and Pharisees. He goes on to say in verse 34 that since they were a brood of poisonous deceivers, He would "send unto [them] prophets, and wise men, and scribes."

1. The identity of those being sent

   Why did Christ say He would send prophets, wise men, and scribes? They were Jewish titles; prophets would be preachers, wise men would be teachers, and scribes would be writers. Even though He was pronouncing final judgment on the religious leaders, He wasn't through sending them messengers from God.

2. The intent for their being sent

   The Lord wasn't sending preachers, teachers, and writers to the false religious leaders so that they would have another chance to believe but so that they would have more opportunities to reject God and pile upon themselves a greater weight of guilt. What a fearful statement! Christ says at the end of verse 34, "Some of them ye shall kill and crucify, and some of them shall ye scourge in your synagogues, and persecute them from city to city, that upon you may come all the righteous blood shed upon the earth." The Lord wanted those who were already guilty to become even more guilty so that they would bear the full weight of their sin.

   The Jewish terms *prophet*, *wise men*, and *scribes* were used in Matthew 23:34 because Matthew's gospel was predominantly directed toward the Jewish people. Christ's use of those terms made His point clear to the scribes and Pharisees. He said more messengers would be sent from God and that the Jewish religious leaders would kill them. He knew that the nation of Israel as a whole would not believe them. A small number of people did believe them; three thousand accepted Christ on the day of Pentecost in Acts 2. But for the most part, the nation of Israel and the religious leaders would kill the messengers and thereby become worthy of greater judgment.

God is a God of judgment and vengeance. We must not forget that. The Lord has frequently used His prophets to preach judgment. When a person hears the gospel, it is a message that leads to salvation—or to judgment. The more often a person receives the message, the more it becomes a message of grace; the more a person rejects the message, the more it brings judgment upon him. Luke 12:48 says, "Unto whomsoever much is given, of him shall be much required." A person who rejects Christ is better off if he's heard the gospel only once and not many times.

Can God Be Glorified Even When People Reject Him?

1. 2 Corinthians 2:14-17

In verse 14 Paul says, "Thanks be unto God, who always causeth us to triumph in Christ, and maketh manifest the savor of his knowledge by us in every place." He was saying he was thankful that no matter where he preached, he always triumphed—regardless of the response. Every time a preacher gives the gospel, he's victorious because the message accomplishes the purpose God designed for it. And the purpose is not only that some might become saved, but also that others might become more guilty. When a person becomes saved, God is glorified because of His grace; and when a person rejects Christ, God is equally glorified because of His judgment.

In 2 Corinthians 2:15 Paul continues, "We are unto God a sweet savor of Christ, in them that are saved, and in them that perish." Was Paul saying it's a sweet taste to God when people perish? It may be hard for us to understand, but God is as much revealed in His glory through the expression of His judgment as He is in the expression of His grace. God isn't just a gracious God of love, kindness, and mercy; He is also a holy God of judgment and wrath against evil. If men choose to be evil, God will be glorified in their condemnation just as He is glorified in the conversion of those who choose to believe in Christ.

Verses 16-17 say, "To the one we are the savor of death unto death; and to the other, the savor of life unto life. . . . For we are not as many, who corrupt the word of God." Paul and his fellow preachers didn't alter the message. They knew they triumphed every time they spoke the truth because they knew God would be glorified either through His grace or through His holy judgment. And God, by being glorified in both ways, reveals Himself fully as He is.

91

2. Revelation 22:11

Near the end of all that God has to say to man through His Word, we read, "He that is unjust, let him be unjust still; and he that is filthy, let him be filthy still; and he that is righteous, let him be righteous still; and he that is holy, let him be holy still" (Rev. 22:11). God was saying that when the end comes, if you are unjust and filthy, let it be so forever. He will be glorified by judging the ungodly. And you are righteous and godly, let it be so forever, for God will be glorified through that as well.

3. Romans 9:21-23

The apostle Paul says in Romans 9 that God has the right to do whatever He wants: "Hath not the potter power over the clay, of the same lump to make one vessel unto honor, and another unto dishonor?" (v. 21). The potter can choose to do what he wants to with the vessels he makes. Verses 22-23 continue, "What if God, although willing to demonstrate His wrath and to make His power known, endured with much patience vessels of wrath prepared for destruction? And He did so in order that He might make known the riches of His glory upon vessels of mercy" (NASB). If God wants to display His wrath and power against sin on vessels of wrath destined for destruction, He has the right to do so. He can also show the riches of His glory on the vessels of mercy as well. God has to be seen in His fullness, and He is glorified just as much in His wrath against ungodliness as He is in His grace toward believers.

B. The Confirmation of Israel's Rejection

1. The prophecy

God said He would send preachers, teachers, and writers to the Jewish religious leaders but not so that they might become saved. All the messengers from God would be killed, scourged, and persecuted, thereby filling up the cup of wrath and bringing judgment against the nation of Israel.

Jesus said regarding the messengers from God, "Some of them ye shall kill and crucify, and some of them shall ye scourge in your synagogues" (v. 34). The word *kill* probably refers to the Jewish tradition of stoning a person to death, and the word *crucify* speaks of the Roman method of execution by nailing a person to a cross. Jesus was crucified by the Jewish leaders through Roman executioners. Stephen was stoned. Many other men of God were persecuted and killed. We have no way of knowing how many, for historians didn't document every death. Some of those who weren't killed were brought close to death through scourging. Paul himself was scourged and beaten with rods (2 Cor. 11:24-25). Christ also says in Matthew 23:34 that the religious leaders would chase godly men from city to city. Paul did that before he became a Christian (Acts 8:1-4; 9:1-2). Some of the cities where persecution took place were Antioch of Pisidia (Acts 13:45, 50), Iconium (14:1-2), Lystra (14:19), Thessalonica (17:5), Berea (17:13), Corinth (18:12), Jerusalem (21:27; 23:12), and Caesarea (24:1-9). The believers in the early church were constantly persecuted by the false spiritual leaders of Israel, who sought to stamp out the gospel of Christ.

2. The purpose

Jesus told the Jewish religious leaders they would fill the cup of God's wrath by killing and persecuting His messengers, so that upon them would "come all the righteous blood shed upon the earth" (Matt. 23:35). The Greek text of verse 35 begins with the word *hopōs*, which means "purpose." The purpose of God's sending preachers, teachers, and writers to the Jewish leaders was so that they might commit the final act of atrocity against the righteous by massacring the Savior Himself and His followers, thereby bringing about certain judgment.

Now God didn't declare judgment on the religious leaders in Matthew 23 because He willed them to be lost. Second Peter 3:9 says that the Lord is "not willing that any should perish, but that all should come to repentance." Men bring judgment upon themselves when they reject the Lord Jesus Christ. Only then will they experience God's wrath.

C. The Comprehensiveness of Israel's Rejection

1. The principle of cumulative guilt

The longer a person rejects the Lord in the face of learning more and more about Him, the greater his guilt will become. Thus the rejectors who were alive in Christ's time have greater guilt than anyone who ever lived before them. It's true that the Old Testament saints had God's law, but the people in Christ's time had both the law and the presence of the Messiah. They heard the teachings of John the Baptist, Jesus, and the apostles. They also should have learned from the judgment God poured out on those who killed the prophets of the Old Testament era. So the religious leaders of Christ's time had accumulated revelation and lessons from history, but they failed to learn from any of it.

a) The accountability of the religious leaders

(1) The explanation about their accountability

How can one generation be held responsible for all the righteous blood shed over several generations? One reason is that it rejected the full light of revelation in Christ. They also hadn't learned from all the lessons of their history. And just as you can see how Israel was filling the cup of God's wrath, you can see how the United States is filling up its cup. The generation alive today is more guilty of their wrongdoing than their ancestors because they have the accumulated testimony of God's truth. The Lord's wrath will break on the generation that finally fills the cup to the brim. That's what happened to Israel shortly after Christ died. A generation that duplicates the sins of past generations and rejects the revelation of God brings upon itself a more profound judgment.

(2) The extent of their accountability

Jesus said that upon the heads of the scribes and Pharisees would come "all the righteous blood shed upon the earth, from the blood of righteous Abel unto the blood of Zechariah, son of Barachiah, whom [they] slew between the temple and the altar" (Matt. 23:35). When someone kills a righteous person, he obviously shows that he rejects God's truth. That's one of the worst sins a person can commit. Our Lord was telling the scribes and Pharisees that they were going to suffer a just punishment for all the righteous blood that had been shed. The first righteous man killed was Abel. Cain couldn't stand the purity of his brother. If a society stoops to the level of killing righteous people, it will do so because it can't tolerate righteousness.

Christ includes in Matthew 23:35 all those murdered between Abel and the last Old Testament martyr, Zechariah the son of Barachiah. There's much discussion today about who Zechariah was. Some people say he was the Zechariah referred to in 2 Chronicles 24:20-21. But that man was the son of Jehoiada. Also, he was alive during the reign of King Joash, which was around 800 B.C. That's a long time before the end of the Old Testament era. Yet some people think he's the one Jesus was referring to because he was stoned to death in the Temple court for rebuking King Joash, who was tolerating idolatry in Israel. They think Jesus mistakenly attributed the wrong name to Zechariah's father. Bible critics try to use this example to say Jesus was prone to error from time to time and that we can't always trust the Bible.

Is that a satisfactory explanation of who Zechariah son of Barachiah was? I think not. There is a Zechariah son of Barachiah in the Bible—the prophet who wrote the book of Zechariah (Zech. 1:1). By the way, there are more than twenty other Zechariahs in the Bible. Only God knows how many more there were who weren't mentioned. So Jesus wasn't referring in Matthew 23:35 to Zechariah son of Jehoiada—the man who was killed about 800 B.C. for being righteous. There was another man later on who happened to have the name Zechariah, who was the son of Barachiah and who was murdered because he was righteous. Although the murder isn't recorded in Scripture, Jesus' listeners knew what He was talking about. So throughout history, the nation of Israel was guilty of killing the righteous messengers of God. Jesus also makes that point clear in Matthew 21:33-41, where He tells the parable of the landowner whose servants (the messengers of God) were killed by the tenants living on the land (the Jewish religious leaders).

I believe the Zechariah Jesus speaks of in Matthew 23:35 is none other than the prophet Zechariah who lived at the end of the Old Testament era, about 580 to 570 B.C. Thus Jesus was accurate when He said the first Old Testament martyr of righteousness was Abel, and the last one was Zechariah son of Barachiah.

b) The animosity of the religious leaders

There were probably quite a few righteous people killed in the Temple area. The Jewish religious leaders tried to kill Paul there (Acts 21:27-31). The most likely reason that righteous people were killed in the Temple area was that that was where the contrast between the unrighteous and righteous came into sharpest focus. There were unrighteous religious leaders running the Temple, and whenever a righteous person came along who threatened the security of the false religious leaders, he was killed. There were probably several times when Christ Himself could have been killed in the Temple. And Zechariah the son of Barachiah was only one of many who died as a martyr because He spoke the truth of God.

c) The accusation against the religious leaders

In addressing the scribes and Pharisees in Matthew 23:35, Jesus refers to Zechariah as one "whom ye slew." Some of the religious leaders were probably thinking, "Wait a minute. We weren't there when

Zechariah was slain. We didn't kill him." But the Lord considered the religious leaders to be as guilty as their fathers. The cup of wrath had been cumulatively filling up through many generations. The guilt of the religious leaders' rejection was increased by the accumulation of previous warnings to Israel. They had so much information about how God wanted them to live, yet they were still filling up the cup of wrath to the brim. That's why Jesus said they were guilty of all the blood shed from Abel to Zechariah. He said they were just as guilty as Cain, those who killed Zechariah, and everyone in between.

2. The promise to the current generation

Our Lord says in Matthew 23:36, "Verily I say unto you, All these things shall come upon this generation." All the guilt from the righteous blood shed up to that time came upon the nation of Israel. There is parallel in the vision the apostle John had of the final, worldwide false church—the harlot mystery Babylon, the great prostitute, the false religion of the Tribulation era—for he says in Revelation 17:6 that he saw her "drunk with the blood of the saints, and with the blood of the martyrs of Jesus." The worldwide false religion of the Tribulation period will accumulate the guilt of our time. So, the scribes and Pharisees would soon have all the guilt from past slayings piled upon them.

Jesus said God's wrath would be poured out "upon this generation." Which generation was He talking about? The people with whom He was talking. He was saying that the nation of Israel would soon face judgment. The cup would be filled when the Jewish religious leaders killed Christ, His apostles, and the people of the early church.

A Story with a Sad Ending

Jesus was crucified shortly after the incident recorded in Matthew 23. True to His word, in A.D. 70, God's judgment came upon Israel. That judgment was a physical reality that symbolized the eternal judgment that will come later upon those who rejected Christ. The judgment poured out on Israel in A.D. 70 is still being poured out today and will continue until the day when the Jewish nation as a whole recognizes Jesus as their Messiah. But the judgment in A.D. 70 was severe; Luke called that period of time "the days of vengeance" (Luke 21:22).

In A.D. 66, a Jewish revolution broke out against Rome. The Israelites had taken as much of the oppression from Rome as they could handle. There were people from a Jewish sect known as the Zealots, who went around with daggers hidden in their cloaks, and they would stab Roman soldiers. They were the terrorists of their time; they went about assassinating people and causing problems. The Zealots lived in the hills and would stage frequent raids on the Romans. Finally in A.D. 66, the skirmishes erupted into a full-scale revolt. Rome struck back by first slaughtering many Jewish people in Galilee. Eventually Titus, the son of Roman emperor Vespasian, besieged the city of Jerusalem with an army of more than eighty thousand men. The Jews laughed at them and mocked them, refusing to surrender. Later on war broke out, and the horrors of what followed are incredible.

The Romans had the Jews trapped inside the city. Any Jew caught outside the city walls was killed outright or crucified. Those Jews within the walls could look out and see crucified Jews all around the city. The Romans stripped the nearby hills of trees to make war machines. They built great siege machines that could catapult huge boulders over the walls of the city, crushing the buildings and people inside. Battering rams and other weapons were made from the wood of trees and bushes in the surrounding area. Because the Romans used wood, the Jews were able to burn many of their weapons. That made the Romans go into the surrounding hillsides to get even more trees to make new weapons. For months, the forests all around Jerusalem were being stripped as the siege went on.

Many problems began to develop inside the city. There was internal strife among the Jews, and some of them began killing each other. Because Jerusalem had been sealed off by the Romans, the people were slowly being starved. Thousands died as a result, and an unbearable stench began to rise from within the city. Jewish historian Josephus, who witnessed this tragedy, said many of the dead bodies were thrown over the walls just to get rid of the stench (*Wars* v.xii.3).

Eventually the Temple itself was destroyed by fire. By about August of A.D. 70 the Roman soldiers went into the Temple and lifted their own banners in the Holy Place and made sacrifices to their false gods. Titus then ordered that the whole city of Jerusalem be razed. It was completely leveled, and all that remained was a small part of the western wall, known today as the Wailing Wall. Josephus said that as a result of the siege, 1,100,000 Jews were killed and 97,000 taken captive (*Wars* vi.ix.3).

Jesus warned the nation of Israel that judgment was imminent. It came, and it came quickly. That's how God feels about the rejection of His truth and His Son.

Focusing on the Facts

1. Why is it ironic that the Jewish people rejected the Messiah (see p. 84)?
2. In Scripture, the image of a cup being filled to the brim is used in connection with what (see p. 86)?
3. What was Jesus telling the scribes and Pharisees to do when He said, "Fill up, then, the measure of your fathers" (Matt. 23:32; see pp. 86-87)?
4. How does Jesus characterize the Jewish religious leaders in Matthew 23:33? How does that characterization tie in with Jesus' statement, "How can ye escape the damnation of hell" (Matt. 23:33; see pp. 88-89)?
5. What was Jesus going to do as a result of the Jewish leaders' iniquity? What was His intent in doing that (Matt. 23:34-36; see p. 90)?
6. Summarize what Paul is saying in 2 Corinthians 2:14-17 (see p. 91).
7. Why do those who rejected Christ in the New Testament era have a greater guilt than those who rejected God in the Old Testament era (see p. 94)?

8. Why might many righteous people have been killed by the Jewish religious leaders in the Temple area (see p. 96)?
9. According to Matthew 23:36, when did Jesus say God's wrath would be poured out on Israel (see p. 97)?
10. How did God's wrath manifest itself when it finally did come in A.D. 70 (see pp. 97-99)?

Pondering the Principles

1. The people who heard Jesus' message in Matthew 23 were probably surprised to hear Jesus tell the Jewish religious leaders that God would soon pour out His wrath on them. They seemed so pious, and no one would have expected them to be the recipients of God's judgment. Yet God was angry with them because their religion was external and ritualistic, whereas God wants internal transformation and wholehearted commitment. First Samuel 16:7 says, "The Lord seeth not as man seeth; for man looketh on the outward appearance, but the Lord looketh on the heart." Are the things of your heart and your outward behavior consistent with each other? It's easy to focus more on external actions and let your internal commitment to the Lord grow lax. Ask God to help you make sure your heart is pure, and pray that your thoughts, words, and action will all reflect a true commitment to God.

2. In Matthew 23, our Lord severely condemns false spiritual leaders. What words does He have for the righteous? Read and enjoy what He has to say in Proverbs 11:18, Colossians 3:23-24, 2 Timothy 4:7-8, and 1 Peter 1:3-9.

6

Jesus' Last Words to Israel— Part 2

Outline

Introduction
A. The Record of Israel's Suffering
 1. During the Roman and Byzantine empires
 2. During the Crusades in Europe
  a) The attempt to convert the Jews
  b) The accusation against the Jews
  c) The antagonism toward the Jews
   (1) In England
   (2) In France
 3. During the Middle Ages
  a) The compounded distrust of the Jews
  b) The continued dispersion of the Jews
 4. During the current era
  a) The Dreyfus affair
  b) The holocaust
B. The Reason for Israel's Suffering

Review
 I. The Imminent Condemnation (vv. 34-36)
 A. The Consequence of Israel's Rejection
 B. The Confirmation of Israel's Rejection
 C. The Comprehensiveness of Israel's Rejection

Lesson
II. The Intense Compassion (vv. 37-38)
 A. The Cry of Jesus

　　B. The Characterization of the Jews
　　　　1. The proclamation
　　　　2. The picture
　　C. The Compassion of Jesus
　　　　1. The proclamation
　　　　2. The picture
　　D. The Choice of the Jews
　　　　1. The proclamation
　　　　2. The pictures
　　　　　　a) Matthew 22
　　　　　　b) Luke 14
　　E. The Condemnation by Jesus
　　　　1. The proclamation
　　　　2. The picture
III. The Insured Conversion (v. 39)
　　A. The Departure from Israel
　　B. The Deliverance of Israel
　　　　1. The prerequisite
　　　　2. The prophecy
　　　　　　a) The future conviction of Israel
　　　　　　b) The future conversion of Israel
　　　　3. The promise

Conclusion

Introduction

Outside of God, no one could possibly have a greater love and compassion for the nation Israel than a truly committed Christian. Some of my favorite people are Jewish: Jesus, the apostle Paul, Peter, Moses, Abraham, and some of my friends at Grace Community Church. The Jewish people were specially chosen by God, and I have a great sense of compassion over their plight. They experience tremendous distress because they believe they are the covenant people of God, yet they don't understand why it seems they are under a curse instead of blessing. They believe they are unique and see themselves as great humanitarians but wonder why they are always being oppressed, persecuted, and massacred.

A. The Record of Israel's Suffering

I have visited the land of Israel, and everywhere are signs that the Jewish people have known century after century of difficulty. You can see today the remnants of the western wall of Jerusalem from when the city was razed in A.D. 70 by the Romans. In other parts of the country you can see the remnants of other wars, both ancient and recent. The ruins range from the rubble of an old city to an overturned tank in the desert. Battles are still raging to this day in that part of the world. The Israelites have suffered as no other nation in history.

It's interesting to notice that despite such persecution over the centuries, God has preserved the Jewish race. They've never been completely wiped out; they haven't lost their identity through intermarriage. They keep perpetuating themselves, yet they are continually being chastened. Why? The Jews cry out that question to a heaven that never seems to answer. They wonder, *If we are the covenant people to whom God granted His laws and through whom the Messiah would come, then why have we suffered so much?*

1. During the Roman and Byzantine empires

The current dilemma facing the Jewish people began with the destruction of Jerusalem in A.D. 70. The Roman general Titus Vespasian besieged the city, and before the siege was over, more than one million Jews died, according to Josephus. Two years earlier, the Gentiles in Caesarea had slain about twenty thousand Jews and sold many more thousands into slavery (Josephus, *Wars* ii.xviii.1). From that time on, for the last two thousand years, the Jewish people have known tremendous suffering.

Around A.D. 70, the inhabitants of a city in Syria killed over thirteen thousand Jews by slitting their throats (*Wars* ii.xviii.2-3). Three centuries later, Roman emperor Theodosius II developed a legal code containing anti-Semitic viewpoints that said the Jewish people were inferior to others. Unfortunately, Theodosius's legal code penetrated all Western law, so from that time on anti-Jewish feelings became established in much of Western culture. In A.D. 630, Byzantine emperor Heraclius banished the Jews from Jerusalem, where they had begun to resettle.

2. During the Crusades in Europe

The persecution of the Jewish people took on even greater proportions during the Crusades in Europe. The first Crusade began in 1096. The Crusades were supposed to be holy wars by so-called Christians in Western Europe. I use the word *Christian* loosely because those people were not Christians in the true biblical sense but only in the name of religion. The crusaders decided to march to the Holy Land and recapture it from the pagan Turks who possessed it. The crusaders believed that the Turks were abusing Christian pilgrims and desecrating what were designated as holy places.

One fear the crusaders had was that the Jewish people would also want to lay claim to the Holy Land once the crusaders took it from the Turks. To prevent that from happening, the crusaders massacred all the Jews they encountered across Europe. They said they were doing that in the name of Christ, and thus you can understand why the Jews dislike Christianity. Even the word *crusade* has an evil connotation to the Jewish mind.

a) The attempt to convert the Jews

Whenever the crusaders came to a town that had a Jewish settlement, they would give the people two choices: convert to Christianity and be publicly baptized, or die. Many Jews chose death, and those who didn't converted only to spare their lives. Some of the Jewish leaders didn't like the false conversions and told their people they were better off dead. After a while, the Jews in many towns and villages began to commit suicide when they heard the crusaders were approaching. Sadly, they were guilty of no crime. In one particular village, some of the Jewish women and young girls decided they would rather die than profess conversion. So they tied rocks to their garments and went to a nearby river to drown. They didn't want to be humiliated by the crusaders.

b) The accusation against the Jews

The Jews were accused of crucifying Christian children and drinking their blood to celebrate Passover. They were accused of many horrible things. In the city of Worms, which later became famous because of Martin Luther, a group of Jews refused to be baptized and were murdered. Their corpses were dragged from one end of the city to the other to desecrate the bodies. During a crusade in 1236, the crusaders went into the regions of Anjou and Poitou and trampled three thousand Jews under their horses' hooves. And the worst was yet to come.

c) The antagonism toward the Jews

(1) In England

By the time King Edward I came into power in 1239, the Jewish people had been scattered all over Europe. They were safe in England until a Dominican monk decided to study the Hebrew Scriptures in order to convert Jews to Roman Catholicism. In the process, he became converted to Judaism and was circumcised. The Roman Catholic church was furious, and the Dominicans felt they had been betrayed and disgraced. They sought vengeance and had the Jews expelled from Cambridge.

Jews were accused of counterfeiting coins and other crimes. They were hanged, exiled, or made to wear badges of some kind that indicated they were Jews. In London, some Jews had their arms and legs tied to horses that were sent off in opposite directions. The remnants of the bodies were then hanged on the gallows for all the town to see.

(2) In France

Around A.D. 1290, the king of England decreed that any Jews remaining in England were to be expelled. They fled into other parts of Europe, including France. The French people had already expelled them under the reign of Louis IX, but later on began to allow them to live there again. However the Jewish people were required to wear a red or yellow cloth badge on their garments to identify themselves. Unfortunately, France didn't allow the Jews to stay for long. About fifteen years after their expulsion from England, Philip the Fair expelled more than one hundred thousand Jewish people from France.

3. During the Middle Ages

   a) The compounded distrust of the Jews

   When the Black Plague spread across Europe in the fourteenth century and killed tens of thousands, the Jews were blamed for it. In France they were accused of poisoning water wells, thereby being responsible for the Black Death. So again, Jews were persecuted and killed. In one town a synagogue filled with people was burned to the ground. As a result of the persecution, the Jews fled farther east into the regions now known as Poland and the Soviet Union. Many Jewish people still live in those countries today.

   b) The continued dispersion of the Jews

   Poland became a homeland for many of the Jews. It was there that they established Talmudic schools and seminaries. Eventually they came into great conflict with the Roman Catholic church and began to be persecuted again. Later on the Jews helped the nobility of Poland and the Jesuits to suppress the rising threat of the Cossacks. But the Cossacks won the ensuing war and took out their vengeance on the Jews by massacring them.

   Some Jewish people escaping persecution in various regions of Europe settled in Spain. Persecution broke out there, leading one Jewish poet to say that Spain was the hell of the Jews. The two who stirred the greatest persecution upon the Jews were King Ferdinand and Queen Isabella—the monarchs who allowed Columbus to sail west over the Atlantic and come to America. They established the Spanish Inquisition in 1478, which included finding out the names of dead people who had converted to Judaism, digging up the graves to desecrate the bodies, and then confiscating the property of the heirs in an attempt to discourage people from converting. A mark depicting a series of flaming crosses had to be worn by every Jew. Finally in 1492, when Columbus sailed west, the Jews were sent east out of Spain. Some of them went to the Soviet Union, where they are still persecuted today.

In the middle of the seventeenth century, the first persecution broke out in Poland after two hundred years of peaceful existence. The German states also began to massacre Jews, reviving the slander that the Jews used the blood of Christian children for their Passover. The German Catholic church said the Jews took knives and stabbed the host of the mass until blood poured forth—to them that was like stabbing the body of Christ.

4. During the current era

   a) The Dreyfus affair

   Anti-Semitism has dominated Western civilization, continuing on up through our time. In 1894 a Jewish officer in the French army was humiliated as a traitor simply because he was Jewish. That action was used to remove the Jewish officers from all the high-ranking positions in the French army.

   b) The holocaust

   In spite of all the persecution and massacres through the centuries, approximately 20 million Jewish people were living in Europe by the time World War II began. During the war, Hitler exterminated nearly 6 million Jews in the great holocaust. But this time the persecution was based not on religion but on race. Hitler sought to eliminate the Jewish people because he believed they were an inferior race.

107

Even though God has allowed many Jews to die, He will not allow them to be exterminated. Unfortunately, secular society picked up the legacy of anti-Semitism and persists in expressing that ugly sin. The Jewish people still suffer today. (For documentation and further information on anti-Semitism, see Richard E. Gade's *A Historical Survey of Anti-Semitism* [Grand Rapids: Baker, 1981].)

B. The Reason for Israel's Suffering

Why have the Jewish people suffered so much? That is a question the Jews continue to ask. Matthew 23:37-38 holds the key: Jesus said, "O Jerusalem, Jerusalem, thou that killest the prophets, and stonest them who are sent unto thee, how often would I have gathered thy children together, even as a hen gathereth her chickens under her wings, and ye would not! Behold, your house is left unto you desolate." What did He mean when He said, "Your house is left unto you desolate"? He was saying that no longer would God plow and cultivate the nation of Israel. No longer would He water them, prune them, and take care of them. No one would protect them; God would leave them to the elements.

Jesus' warning in Matthew 23:38 is similar to the warning Isaiah gave to Israel before the Babylonian captivity. God planted Israel as a noble vine in a fertile hill. He put a moat around them to protect them. He did all He could to cause them to bring forth sweet grapes, but they brought forth sour berries (Isa. 5:1-2). God's judgment is stated in verses 5-6: "I will tell you what I will do to my vineyard: I will take away its hedge, and it shall be eaten up; and break down its wall, and it shall be trampled down. And I will lay it waste; it shall not be pruned, nor digged, but there shall come up briers and thorns; I will also command the clouds that they rain no rain upon it." In the two thousand years since Jesus' statement in Matthew 23:38, the nation of Israel has had to live without God's protection. That's why the people have suffered. God has preserved them as a people, but He has generally left them unprotected from all the holocausts the world could bring to bear.

Why did God remove His protecting hand from the Israelites? Jesus says in Matthew 23:37, "O Jerusalem . . .

how often would I have gathered thy children together even as a hen gathereth her chickens under her wings, and ye would not!" The Jewish people rejected their Messiah. That's why God stopped protecting them.

If the Jews had received Christ, the kingdom of God would have come to earth. But because they rejected Him, they have suffered ever since. Jesus came to bring His kingdom, yet His people rejected Him, thus forfeiting the kingdom. Instead of entering into the blessing of God, the Lord removed His blessings from them and left them to the fate of an evil world. Consequently the Jewish people have suffered immeasurably. Paul says in 1 Corinthians 16:22, "If any man love not the Lord Jesus Christ, let him be Anathema [i.e., cursed]." God gave the Israelites incredible privileges. With those privileges came tremendous responsibility. Because they rejected Christ, the Lord left them desolate.

Review

Verses 37-39 close Jesus' sermon in Matthew 23. It's the last sermon our Lord gave in public. He directed it against the false spiritual leaders who led the nation of Israel to reject Him. That doesn't mean the people were less guilty for their rejection; it's just that the religious leaders further encouraged their rejection. So Jesus speaks out furiously against those leaders in Matthew 23. And His sermon ends in grief. He laments because God was going to judge Israel by removing His protecting hand and letting Satan attack the nation. Although God has taken away His protection from other nations, it is worse for Israel because Satan wants to exterminate that nation more than any other. They are a part of God's sovereign plan, and Satan wants to thwart what God is doing. Satan wants to get rid of the Jewish people so that Christ can never inherit them and fulfill God's promise that many of them will be redeemed someday (Rom. 11:26).

Even though God had to judge Israel, His heart was full of grief. In Ezekiel 33:11 He says, "I have no pleasure in the death of the wicked." In Jeremiah 13 God says that if the Israelites didn't glorify Him, He would weep bitterly (vv. 16-17).

I. THE IMMINENT CONDEMNATION (vv. 34-36; see pp. 89-99)

A. The Consequence of Israel's Rejection (see pp. 89-92)

In Matthew 23:34-36 Jesus is saying to the scribes and Pharisees, "Because you have rejected the Messiah and killed all the prophets of the past, you have cumulatively rejected all God's revelation. You know the Old Testament Scriptures, you heard the preaching of John the Baptist, and you saw My ministry. You've rejected it all. You've almost filled the cup of God's wrath. Soon it will be filled, and God's judgment will pour out on you." It took a number of centuries for the cup to be filled, and it is now being poured out with centuries of chastening.

B. The Confirmation of Israel's Rejection (see pp. 92-93)

C. The Comprehensiveness of Israel's Rejection (see pp. 94-99)

Why are the people Jesus is talking with in Matthew 23 guilty of the sins of their ancestors? Because they knew about the sins of the past and didn't learn from them. They inherited their ancestors' guilt. Not only did they refuse to listen to Jesus and the apostles, but they also didn't listen to John the Baptist and the other prophets before him. So they had cumulative guilt. They had rejected full light and revelation. They were among those "who were once enlightened, and have tasted of the heavenly gift, and were made partakers of the Holy Spirit, and have tasted the good word of God, and the powers of the age to come" (Heb. 6:4-5). But in spite of the full revelation they had, the Jewish religious leaders blasphemed the Holy Spirit by saying Christ was from Satan (Matt. 12:24-32). Thus the Lord says in Matthew 23:36, "All these things shall come upon this generation." God's judgment was going to be poured out on the generation with which Christ was speaking. The beginning of that outpouring occurred in A.D. 70 with the destruction of Jerusalem, and it continues on to this day.

The persecution the Jewish people endure will become worse. God's protective hand is still removed from them, and Satan is still assailing them. The worst is yet to come in the time known as the Great Tribulation, or the time of Jacob's trouble

(Jer. 30:7). Now the fact that the nation of Israel is being chastised by God, and that Satan is doing all he can to destroy them, doesn't mean individual Jews can't come to Christ. They can, and they will. God has always had a remnant who were faithful to Him (Rom. 11:5). Some Jewish people recognize Jesus as the Messiah, but for the nation as a whole is coming a terrible time of judgment.

Lesson

II. THE INTENSE COMPASSION (vv. 37-38)

In Matthew 23:37-38 is an outpouring of grief equal to the outpouring of wrath in the preceding verses. It is a climax of great compassion. It provides for us an essential balance and understanding of the character of God and Christ. Jesus has already stated furious words of judgment, and now He shares words of grief. God never rejoices in punishment; He doesn't gloat over the doom of people. He grieves over those who must be punished.

A. The Cry of Jesus

Matthew 23:37 begins, "O Jerusalem, Jerusalem." There's a certain pathos in the repetition of the name *Jerusalem*. Christ's sorrow is apparent in that phrase. In Luke 19 we read of a similar incident. Verses 41-42 say, "When [Jesus] was come near, he beheld the city, and wept over it, saying, If thou hadst known, even thou, at least in this thy day, the things which belong unto thy peace! But now they are hidden from thine eyes." That happened on Monday of the Passion Week—the day of His triumphal entry into the city. He wept when He saw the city and said, "If only you knew who was here visiting you!" It may well be that He wept again on Wednesday when He said, "O Jerusalem, Jerusalem" (Matt. 23:37). He lamented because the Jews were about to have God's protective care removed from them and therefore be exposed to Satan.

In Scripture, the repetition of a phrase or a name can indicate great emotion. In Luke 10:41 Jesus says, "Martha, Martha," and in Luke 22:31 He says, "Simon, Simon."

111

Both times He spoke from great concern. In Acts 9 Christ says from heaven, "Saul, Saul, why persecutest thou me?" (v. 4). Another good example appears in 2 Samuel 18:33, where it is recorded that King David cried in anguish, "O my son Absalom, my son, my son Absalom! Would God I had died for thee, O Absalom, my son, my son!"

B. The Characterization of the Jews

1. The proclamation

Matthew 23:37 says, "Jerusalem, thou that killest the prophets, and stonest them who are sent unto thee." What a characterization of what was supposed to be the holy city—the city of God! Jesus didn't say it was loveliest among all the cities of the earth. He didn't call Jerusalem the golden city; He called it the city of murderers.

Jesus said of the Jewish religious leaders, "[Thou] killest the prophets, and stonest them who are sent unto thee." Those words were so accurate: the religious leaders were about to kill Jesus, who was the supreme prophet, and they would soon stone Stephen to death (Acts 7:59-60). They had been killing God's messengers all along, and they would continue to do so. As Christ says in Matthew 23:35, the ancestors of the Jewish leaders had killed Zechariah between the Temple and the altar. Instead of listening to the prophets, they killed them.

2. The picture

In Matthew 21, Jesus tells the scribes and Pharisees that they were like a group of tenant farmers who leased a vineyard, yet killed the servants who were sent to collect payment. After all the servants were killed, the owner of the vineyard sent his son to collect payment. The tenant farmers killed him too. So the scribes and Pharisees were killers of those who spoke the truth and represented God. They were murderers of the righteous.

Now you can understand why Israel has suffered for so long. The nation as a whole rejected God. They killed His messengers and stoned some of them. They finally filled the cup of God's wrath to the brim when they executed their

Messiah. Therefore the Lord said, "Your house is left unto you desolate" (Matt. 23:38). He then removed His hand of blessing and allowed them to become subject to Satan's attacks. Their suffering will culminate during the Tribulation when the mouth of the bottomless pit is opened to allow the demons bound within to run rampant across the earth (Rev. 9:1-12). Then Israel will know persecution not only from men but from supernatural demons as well.

C. The Compassion of Jesus

1. The proclamation

After Jesus characterized Jerusalem, He said, "How often would I have gathered thy children together" (v. 37). He wanted to bring the Jewish people into safety. He wanted to protect them; He didn't want to remove His hand of blessing. Jesus wasn't talking just about wanting to protect the people whenever He came to Jerusalem. His heart ached for them all the time. He wanted to bring the Jewish people to Himself throughout His ministry. We see the Lord's compassion for all people in other parts of Scripture as well. In Matthew 11:28 Christ says, "Come unto me, all ye that labor and are heavy laden, and I will give you rest." When the Lord died on the cross, He gathered into His arms the thief next to Him who was willing to believe (Luke 23:42-43). The Lord was always wanting to gather His people and give them protection.

2. The picture

Jesus gives a beautiful illustration of protection in Matthew 23:37. He told the Jews He wanted to gather them "even as a hen gathereth her chickens under her wings." In a farmyard, when a hen sees a chicken hawk flying overhead, she immediately gathers her chicks and protects them. When a storm approaches and the lightning and thunder scare her chicks, she will gather her little ones and give them warmth and security.

The Lord's illustration depicts His great tenderness. He didn't speak to Israel merely in theological terms; He spoke to the people in a personal, intimate way. He wanted to give them security.

D. The Choice of the Jews

1. The proclamation

What was Israel's response? The end of Matthew 23:37 says, "And ye would not!" The Jewish people rejected Jesus' offer of protection.

The Power of Choice

Those who are hard-line Calvinists (who say that a man's decision has no part in his salvation) would have difficulty with Matthew 23:37 because it contradicts their theology. Jesus pointed out that the Israelites' response—their refusal to receive Him—brought about their condemnation. God wanted to protect them, but the Israelites wouldn't let Him. Thus God's sovereignty and man's response are inseparably linked in a person's salvation. Every soul that spends eternity in hell is there because he would not allow God to bring him under His protection.

2. The pictures

a) Matthew 22

In a parable about a wedding feast held by a king, Jesus said the king "sent forth his servants to call them that were bidden to the wedding; and they would not come" (v. 3). Likewise, the people of Israel were called by the Lord, but they refused to come to Him.

b) Luke 14

Jesus said, "A certain man gave a great supper, and bade many. And sent his servant at supper time to say to them that were bidden, Come; for all things are now ready. And they all with one consent began to make excuse. The first said unto him, I have bought a piece of ground, and I must needs go and see it; I pray thee, have me excused. And another said, I have bought five yoke of oxen, and I go to prove them; I pray thee, have me excused. And another said, I have married a wife, and, therefore, I cannot come. So that servant came, and showed his lord these things. Then the master of the house, being angry, said to his servant, Go out quickly into the streets and lanes of the city, and bring in here the poor, and the maimed, and the lame, and the blind" (vv. 16-21). The master decided that if those who were invited didn't want to come, he would invite anyone who wanted to come.

There is no absolute predetermination about a man's fate. Man's choice is as much a part of salvation as is God's sovereignty. Anyone who goes to hell does so because he would not come to the Lord.

E. The Condemnation by Jesus

1. The proclamation

Verse 38 begins, "Behold, your house." The word *behold* indicates His statement is something of a surprise. "Your house" is a reference to the Temple, which symbolized the nation of Israel. Jesus has referred to the Temple as His Father's house in John 2:16, but in verse 38 He says that the Temple is their house. By that time, the false religious leaders had so desecrated the Temple, God removed His presence from it. The term *Ichabod*, which means "the glory is departed," now applied (1 Sam. 4:21). When Jesus said the Temple was no longer God's house, He was saying that God's protection was gone from the Temple, the city, and the nation. In fact, God's house now is the church (1 Tim. 3:15). In Deuteronomy 28:15-68 we read God's stern warning to the Israelites about what would happen if they turned away from Him. They did turn away; therefore they suffered the curses stated in Deuteronomy 28.

So in Matthew 23:38, Christ rejects Israel because Israel rejected Him. Again, that doesn't mean that certain Jewish individuals can't become saved. On the day of Pentecost, three thousand Jews were saved (Acts 2:41). Later on in the book of Acts many more became saved. Jewish people have been acknowledging Christ as the Messiah throughout the church age. God will always have His remnant. Some will become saved, but the nation in general still rejects Christ. Thus God has kept His hand of protection away from it. Jesus said their house would become desolate, and that's what happened.

2. The picture

In Luke 19:43 Jesus tells the Israelites, "The days shall come upon thee, that thine enemies shall cast a trench about thee, and keep thee on every side, and shall lay thee even with the ground, and thy children within thee; and they shall not leave in thee one stone upon another; because thou knewest not the time of thy visitation." That's a prophecy warning of the destruction of Jerusalem in A.D. 70. Because the Jewish people didn't recognize that Jesus was God incarnate, their city would be devastated. Jewish historian Josephus said that the whole city was razed—nothing was left except the prominent towers and the western wall of the city. Because the city had been so completely devastated, he said future visitors would have no reason to believe that the city had ever been inhabited (*Wars* vii.i.1). Since that time, Israel has remained unprotected. That was the divine payoff for their rejection of their Messiah and God's messengers.

III. THE INSURED CONVERSION (v. 39)

A. The Departure from Israel

Jesus says at the beginning of Matthew 23:39, "Ye shall not see me henceforth." He was saying, "I'm leaving now. This is the end. Farewell from your Messiah; your rejection is final." We know that their rejection was final because the religious leaders wanted to kill the apostles when they preached the gospel after Christ's resurrection. Thus Israel refused the grace of salvation when it was offered. The Lord's mission as the Savior of their nation ended for the time being.

Does that mean there's no hope for Israel? If it did, it would mean that many of the promises God made to Israel in the Old Testament would be broken. It would mean we wouldn't be able to trust God's promises anymore. God said He would regather the Jewish people someday and that He would ultimately become their King (Jer. 31:31-34). If Matthew 23:39 simply ended by saying, "Ye shall not see me henceforth," then we would have to rethink what the Old Testament says, as well as change our view on God's character. But Matthew 23:39 does not end there.

B. The Deliverance of Israel

1. The prerequisite

The next word after "henceforth" in Matthew 23:39 is "till." The Jews *will* see the Messiah again—after a certain time. So there is still hope. Something will happen, and then the Jews will see the Lord again. When will that be? Jesus said they wouldn't see Him until they say, "Blessed is he that cometh in the name of the Lord."

In Matthew 21:9, when Jesus rides into Jerusalem in His triumphal entry, the people were hailing Him as the Messiah and saying, "Hosanna to the Son of David! Blessed is he that cometh in the name of the Lord!" The latter phrase comes from Psalm 118:26. It was a cry meant to identify the Messiah. The Messiah was the One who would come in the Lord's name or as a representative of the Lord. So Jesus was saying the Jewish nation wouldn't see Him again until they recognize Him as their Messiah.

2. The prophecy

a) The future conviction of Israel

Will the Jewish people ever recognize Jesus as the Messiah? The book of Zechariah says they will. In Zechariah 12, God says, "It shall come to pass . . . that I will seek to destroy all the nations that come against Jerusalem. And I will pour upon the house of David, and upon the inhabitants of Jerusalem, the Spirit of grace and of supplications; and they shall look upon me whom they have pierced, and they shall mourn for him, as one mourneth for his only son, and shall be in bitterness for him, as one that is in bitterness for his firstborn" (vv. 9-10).

Those verses are saying that when God's cup of wrath is fully poured out, He will once again look with favor upon Jerusalem and destroy the nations that come against Israel. He will pour on Jerusalem the Spirit of grace. The scales will be removed from the eyes of the Jewish people, and they will recognize the Christ whom they once pierced. They will mourn for Him as for an only Son. They will say, "Now we understand why we have suffered throughout history. We mourn, for we have killed the only Son, the Messiah!" (vv. 11-14). Their grief will be overwhelming because God will pour out on them the Spirit of grace and supplication, leading them to cry out to Him for blessing and mercy.

b) The future conversion of Israel

Zechariah 13:1 says, "In that day there shall be a fountain opened to the house of David and to the inhabitants of Jerusalem for sin and uncleanness [i.e., God will wash the nation clean]. And it shall come to pass, in that day, saith the Lord of hosts, that I will cut off the names of the idols out of the land, and they shall no more be remembered; and also I will cause the prophets and the unclean spirit to pass out of the land" (v. 2). God will save His people someday.

In verse 9 God says, "I will bring the third part through the fire, and will refine them as silver is refined, and will test them as gold is tested; they shall call on my name, and I will hear them. I will say, It is my people; and they shall say, The Lord is my God."

When the Jewish people look upon Christ and acknowledge Him as their Messiah—when they say, "Blessed is He that cometh in the name of the Lord"—that's when they will see Him. Zechariah 14:3 says, "Then shall the Lord go forth. . . . And his feet shall stand in that day upon the Mount of Olives, which is before Jerusalem on the east, and the Mount of Olives shall cleave in its midst toward the east and toward the west." When Christ returns, He will descend onto the Mount of Olives. That will happen immediately after the Jewish people recognize Him as their Messiah.

3. The promise

Will Matthew 23:39 come to pass? Will the Jewish people say Christ is their Messiah? The apostle Paul says they will. In Romans 11:11 he writes, "Have they [the Jews] stumbled that they should fall? God forbid." The Jewish people have fallen, but not permanently. Verse 23 continues, "If they abide not still in unbelief, [they] shall be grafted in." Paul had been talking about branches on a tree and was saying that God will graft the broken branch of Israel back onto His tree. Verses 26-27 say, "All Israel shall be saved . . . for this is my covenant unto them, when I shall take away their sins." God will take away their sins someday—that's definite. He has ensured their restoration.

Conclusion

The Lord ended His sermon of condemnation on a note of hope. How does this sermon apply to those of us who are not of Israel? If God chastised and punished His own beloved people Israel, what do you think will happen to you if you reject Christ? Will you fare any better than His people? The lesson everyone can learn from Matthew 23 is that if you don't love the Lord, you are cursed. That principle applies to both nations and individuals. You need to make a choice. The Lord seeks to gather you into the safety of His love and salvation. Will you allow that? He wants to bring you to Himself, but if you won't let Him, you must be left to Satan's devices.

Focusing on the Facts

1. What has God done for the Jewish people despite the persecution they've received over the centuries (see p. 103)?
2. Describe briefly some of the sufferings the Jewish people have endured since the destruction of Jerusalem in A.D. 70. Why have the Jewish people suffered so much (see pp. 103-7)?
3. How did God feel about judging Israel? Support your answer with Scripture (see p. 109).

4. How is Christ's sorrow made apparent in Matthew 23:37 (see p. 111)?
5. How did Jesus characterize the Jews in Matthew 23:37 (see p. 112)?
6. What did Christ want so much to do for the Jewish people? How did He illustrate that (Matt. 23:37; see p. 113)?
7. What was Israel's response to Jesus' desire (see p. 114)?
8. What is significant about the fact that the Lord does not call the Temple "the Father's house" in Matthew 23:38 (see p. 115)?
9. What does Jesus say will happen to Israel in Luke 19:43, and what event fulfilled that prophecy (see p. 116)?
10. What must happen before the Jewish people see Jesus again (see p. 117)?
11. How will they respond when they see Christ again (Zech. 12:9-10; see pp. 117-18)?
12. What verses in Romans verify that the Jewish nation will one day be restored (see p. 119)?

Pondering the Principles

1. Read Nehemiah 9, and describe the kind of patience God showed toward Israel. Why do you think God showed such patience? What are some ways God has been patient with you? Now read Hebrews 12:6-10. What does the Lord do to those whom He loves (v. 6)? Why does He do that (v. 10)? The Lord frequently gives us a second chance when we make a mistake, but He also has the right to chastise us if necessary. Thank God for the patience He has displayed toward you in the past, and ask Him to make you sensitive to learn what you need to when He chastises you.

2. Some people view the God of the Old Testament era as a God of wrath based on the frequency of times He pronounced and enacted judgment upon people, but they fail to realize that He is grieved when men put Him in that position. Memorize 2 Peter 3:9; it's a great verse to use when witnessing to a non-Christian: "The Lord is not slow about His promise, as some count slowness, but is patient toward you, not wishing for any to perish but for all to come to repentance" (NASB).

Scripture Index

Genesis
6:3 — 87

Exodus
13:1-10 — 34
13:11-16 — 34
13:9, 16 — 36

Leviticus
11:4 — 75
11:41-43 — 75
27:30 — 72

Deuteronomy
6:4-9 — 34
6:8 — 36
11:13-21 — 34
11:18 — 36
12:10-11, 17-18 — 72
14:22 — 72-73
14:28-29 — 72
28:15-68 — 115

Numbers
15:37-41 — 37

1 Samuel
4:21 — 115

2 Samuel
18:33 — 111

2 Kings
23:10 — 59

2 Chronicles
24:20-21 — 95
28:3 — 59

Psalms
50:14 — 70
56:12 — 70
61:8 — 70
66:13 — 70
76:11 — 70
118:26 — 117

Isaiah
5:1-2, 5-6 — 108
10:1-2 — 23-24
24:2 — 46
30:10 — 16
51:17 — 86

Jeremiah
5:31 — 46
7:4-7 — 24
7:31 — 59
12:10 — 46
13:16-17 — 109
14:14 — 15
23:21 — 16
23:32 — 16
25:15 — 86
27:15 — 16
28:15 — 16
29:9 — 16
30:7 — 111
31:31-34 — 117

Ezekiel
13:3 — 8
33:11 — 109
34:1-9 — 24-25

Jonah
4:1-3 — 57

Micah
6:8 — 73

Habakkuk
2:16 — 86

Zechariah
1:1 — 95
12:9-14 — 117-18
13:1-2, 9 — 118
14:3 — 118

Matthew
3:5-8 — 52
3:7 — 88-89
5:21-48 — 17
5:34, 37 — 69
6:1-2 — 32
6:5 — 33
6:10-18 — 33
7:15 — 47
9:20 — 37
9:36 — 25
11:28 — 113
11:28-30 — 25
12:20 — 48
12:24-32 — 110
15:14 — 68
16:19 — 54
20:20-21 — 37
20:28 — 41
21:9 — 65, 117
21:12-13 — 66
21:18-22 — 9
21:23—23:39 — 9
21:28—22:14 — 66
21:33-44 — 78, 96
22:3 — 114 — 68
23:1 — 9-13
23:1-12 — 66
23:2 — 11, 14-18
23:2-7 — 14
23:3 — 17-21
23:4 — 21-26, 73

23:5 — 32-37
23:6 — 37-38
23:6-7 — 37-39
23:7 — 38-39
23:8 — 40
23:8-12 — 10, 39-41
23:9 — 40
23:10 — 40
23:11 — 40
23:12 — 41
23:13 — 11, 51-56, 66, 85
23:13-33 — 48, 50, 85
23:13-36 — 9, 65-66
23:14 — 48-49
23:15 — 31, 49, 56-60, 67
23:16 — 68-70
23:16-22 — 85
23:17 — 71
23:18-19 — 71
23:20-22 — 71-72
23:23 — 19, 72-73
23:23-24 — 72-75, 85
23:24 — 75
23:25 — 19
23:25-26 — 75-76, 85
23:27 — 19
23:27-28 — 76-77, 85
23:28 — 19
23:29-32 — 77-78, 86
23:30 — 87
23:31 — 87
23:32 — 86
23:33 — 19, 49, 79, 88-89
23:34 — 89-90, 93
23:34-36 — 110-11
23:35 — 93, 95-96, 112
23:36 — 97
23:37 — 49, 108-9, 111-14
23:37-38 — 108, 111-16
23:37-39 — 66, 109
23:38 — 108, 112, 115
23:39 — 116-19
24:24 — 8
26:39 — 86

Mark
  9:35   41
  12:40   23, 48
  16:15   17

Luke
  10:41   111
  11:39-54   10
  11:52   53-54
  12:48   91
  14:16-21   115
  19:41   50
  19:43   116
  20:47   48
  21:22   98
  22:31   111
  23:42-43   113

John
  2:16   115
  8:44   68
  9:21-24, 30-34   54
  10:1-2   16
  13:27   86
  20:22   17

Acts
  2:41   115
  4:16-18   55
  5:1-2   70
  5:5, 10-11   70
  5:28   10-11
  7:59-60   112
  8:1-4   93
  9:1-2   93
  9:4   111
  13:45, 50   93
  13:50   57
  14:1-2   93
  14:19   93
  16:14   57
  17:4   17
  17:5   93

  17:13   93
  18:7   57
  18:12   93
  20:29   8
  20:29-31   30, 48
  21:27   93
  21:27-31   96
  23:12   93
  24:1-9   93
  28:3-5   88

Romans
  2:17-24   52
  2:19-20   68
  7:22   19
  9:21-23   92
  11:5   111
  11:23   119
  11:26   109
  11:26-27   119

1 Corinthians
  9:17   17
  15:10   79
  16:22   109

2 Corinthians
  2:15-17   91
  11:24-25   93

Galatians
  1:8-9   8, 22
  4:14   64
  5:1   22
  6:12   32

Ephesians
  2:8-9   52
  2:10   19
  3:8   79

Philippians
  2:29-30   64

1 Thessalonians		2 Peter	
2:14-16	55	2:1	20
5:12-13	40, 64	2:3	23, 72
5:17	64	2:10	20
		2:12	20
1 Timothy		2:13	20
3:15	115	2:14	20
4:1	8, 53	2:15	20
4:2	20	2:17	20
4:3	23	2:19	20
4:4	23	3:9	93
4:14	17		
		1 John	
Titus		2:18, 22	8
1:2	68		
		Jude	
Hebrews		8	8, 20
6:4-5	110	10	20
13:7	40	12-13	20
13:17	64	19	33
		23	60
James			
4:10	41	Revelation	
		6:14	25
1 Peter		9:1-12	113
3:7	23	16:19	86
5:2	41	17:6	97
5:5	41	22:11	92
5:7	22-23		